Letters of a Chinese Student at Wellesley 1922–1926

Bing Xin

Translated by
Gail Graham

ISBN: 1511890223
ISBN-13: 978-1511890229

ABOUT BING XIN

Bing Xin was born in China in 1900. She completed her undergraduate studies at a Chinese university and was then awarded a scholarship to Wellesley College. The idea of leaving family and friends and traveling alone to what was truly "the other side of the world" terrified her. She was terribly homesick, and sought comfort in writing. Her letters and essays about her travels and studies in the United States -- including a bout with tubrculosis and a stay in a sanatorium -- were gathered eventually into a book that is considered a classic of modern Chinese literature. Bing Xin continued to write throughout her life, and is sometimes called the "Grandmother of Modern Chinese Literature." She died in 1999.

ABOUT THE TRANSLATOR

Gail Graham is a retired professor and author of eight other books, including two novels and several autobiographical works. She has won a number of literary awards, including Germany's prestigious Buxtehude Bullen. Gail encountered Bing Xin's writings when she was studying Chinese at Melbourne University in Australia, and was struck by the unique beauty of Bing Xin's prose and her intriguing insights into American life in the early 20th century.

July 25, 1923
Beijing

I haven't written anything for several months. Traveling tired me out. But yesterday when I was reading a Chinese newspaper I felt inspired, and the next thing I knew I'd picked up my pen and started to write this letter.

You're thinking, Yes, but why are you writing to us? And what will you write about? So let me begin by introducing myself. I'm just a person like anybody else. But once, I was the same age as you are. And sometimes, I still feel like that ... as if I'm much younger than I really am, as if I'm not much older than you.

Soon I'll leave my home to go to a strange, new place that's nothing at all like China. What will happen to the young "me" that's hidden inside the great, big, "mature" me? That's why I'm writing to you, because I think you can help me.

I'll go so far away, all the way to the other side of the world. Maybe the best part of this journey will be writing to you about the interesting things I see.

I have three little brothers and one of them has studied geography and knows the earth is round. He teases me. "Sister, when you're gone and we're missing you, we'll go out to the garden, poke a bamboo pole down through the middle of the earth and it'll come out on the other side, in

1

your garden. It'll be just like drilling a hole! We'll be able to look down and see one another, and we'll know if you get fat!"

Absurd, isn't it?

My youngest brother keeps asking, "Is the place you're going even further than the front gate?"

Well, how far is it to the other side of the world? Do you think I should tell him that it's much, much further than the front gate?

I'm leaving my mother and father and brothers and everyone I love here in China. I won't be away for very long but even so, the thought of leaving them makes me terribly sad. On windy mornings and rainy evenings, when you're safe and happy with your family and friends all around you, please think of me ... far away across the sea, all alone in a bleak, cold place without anyone to love. Please think of me. If I feel your thoughts I won't be quite so lonely.

I think I'll have lots of spare time, so I'll try to write as often as I can. But if it's sometimes a long time between letters, try to understand. It's the little "me" who is writing these letters. The mature "me" would never do such a thing.

July 28, 1923
Beijing

This is only my second letter, and I probably shouldn't tell you sad stories before you've even had a chance to get to know me! But there's something I've been feeling guilty about for months, and I'd like to get it off my chest.

It happened one evening last spring. It was a quiet evening, just past nine. My little brothers had gone to bed but Mama and Papa were still awake and sitting at our round table reading, chatting and eating fruit. I picked up a book, leaned back in my chair and started to read. It was a peaceful, happy time.

Suddenly, a baby mouse crept out from under the chair and began nibbling at some crumbs on the floor. It was a very, very tiny mouse. It nibbled away, calmly and fearlessly -- and then stopped and looked straight up at me. I was so shocked that I gave a little cry of surprise, and my parents looked up to see what had frightened me. However, being stared at from all sides didn't seem to bother the little mouse a bit. It didn't even try to run away. You could see how little it was in the lamplight, with a long, grey tail, a tiny little body and two bright, glittering little eyes.

But let me tell you what happened next. Without thinking about what I was doing, I made a little tent out of the paper-covered book I'd been reading and put it down over the mouse. To my amazement, it didn't run away! I could actually feel its warm, little body through the paper covers of the book, crouching all curled up and unresisting on the floor.

That wasn't what I expected. I could actually feel his tail, and his tiny little head. Mother said, "Why on earth did you do that? It's such a cute little thing!"

Just then, our cat came running out from behind the screen. Father said, "Quick! Let it go, or the cat will get it"!

Again without thinking about what I was doing, I took the book away. The poor little thing! It didn't even know it was supposed to run! It gave one frightened, little squeak, and then the cat had it!

I cried Stop! at the cat but of course, it didn't. Holding the mouse in its mouth, it darted out past the screen. As I ran after it, I heard the little baby mouse let out a few weak, pathetic squeaks. Then, nothing. Not a sound. From start to finish, the whole thing took less than a minute. Oh, dear! Thinking about that innocent little baby mouse made my heart ache as if I'd been shot.

I sighed. Slowly, Mother put down her book, looked up at me and said, "It really was very tiny, and it was so young it didn't even know how to be afraid. Otherwise, it would have tried to run away. That was probably the first time it was ever out on its own. When it doesn't come home, its poor mother is going to worry."

Doesn't this make you want to cry? When I was your age, that's what I did, if I heard a story like this. But I didn't cry. Instead, I did a terrible thing. I pretended I didn't care. I even smiled.

When it was time to go to bed, I went to my room. By then, that fake, false smile of mine had made the awful thing that I'd done seem even worse. I stood there in the dark for a long time, not knowing what to do. I didn't get undressed. I just leaned against the side of my bed, hugging my pillow. I stayed there like that for about a quarter of an hour – finally, I began to cy.

Although that happened last year, when I'm reading late at night I can see that little mouse come out from under the chair, almost as if it's haunting me! I'd do anything to chase it away. And then I find myself thinking about the little mouse's mother, crying bitter mouse-tears and coming out each night to search for her lost baby.

I think about it whenever I see a cat. I think about it whenever I'm sitting alone, at night. And every time I think about it, my heart aches. Once, I felt so awful that I confessed everything to an adult friend. I was sure she'd say I'd done an awful thing, but I hoped that being "punished" like that might make me feel better. To my amazement, my friend merely laughed. "You are becoming more and more like a baby!" she said. "Carrying on over something no bigger than a pin-prick!"

Shaking her head, she smiled and walked away. So, I gave up. I won't try to tell anyone else about this "thing no bigger than a pin-prick" ... what's the use?

When I was your age, I remember weeping over a cricket with a broken leg, and over a wounded finch. When I was your age, I understood that the cricket and the finch were living creatures and that I was a living creature and that all living creatures were one and the same to God. When I was your age, I never did such awful things, but now that I'm all grown up –

Well, now you know. So it's up to you to decide what sort of person I am.

Sooner or later, all friends must say farewell.

When I returned home a few nights before my departure, it was already dark. There was no electricity. A couple of candles were burning in the room, and as I came through the bamboo curtain into the flickering light, I felt sad and lonely.

When I entered the hall I could hear Mama talking to my younger brothers Han and Jie. Her voice was a continuous murmur but when I came in the curtains swayed, and everyone fell silent. Mama bent her head over her sewing, and Han and Jie stood up, looking disappointed. They stood silently, their hands resting lightly upon the back of the chair, staring into the candlelight.

Haltingly, I began to tell Mama about the farewell dinner I'd attended today. Han and Jie didn't join the conversation, nor did I speak to them.

But when Mama left the room, I asked them what was going on. Han didn't say a word. But at last Jie sighed and said, "Mama says she hates the thought of you leaving and that if you go she'll be … but she doesn't want you to know how she feels …"

For the past few months we'd been very close to one another, but they'd been too soft-hearted and considerate to raise this topic. Hearing this tonight, I was struck dumb.

Suddenly Han murmured, "Jie! Mama says it's wrong to repeat things. What do you think you're doing?"

There was a short silence – and just then, the electricity came on, the light revealing their two, flushed faces.

Xie replied hesitantly, "I thought ... I thought it didn't matter ..."

Han interrupted him. "No, you never think about what you say!

At that, Xie became angry. He felt he'd had enough of his brother's scolding and now he stood up for himself. "You can keep secrets from other people, but how can you keep secrets from your own, eldest sister?"

They glanced unhappily at one another. And as if a silent agreement had been reached, they both bowed their heads.

I just stood there, not knowing what to think.

The electricity went off again. Thank heavens the light was gone! We groped with warm, trembling fingers, tightly holding hands, unable to see the tears brimming in one another's eyes.

*　*　*　*　*

It ended up being a muddled, dazed, and hurried departure. But it wasn't lingering nor was it heartbreaking. My worries had been for nothing.

At midday, I couldn't eat any of the food set out on the table. My little brothers called to me, but I just lay there on my bed in my dressing-gown. Outside I heard Mama say, "Shh! Don't trouble her."

I rallied – that afternoon, several of my brothers' friends came and their noisy play diverted me. They were all gathered around the big lotus pond in the courtyard, splashing water on one another. I ended up getting soaked! Mama had gone to see Aunty, who lives in the west courtyard, so she was out for the afternoon. But she'd told the cook to fix me a bowl of noodles.

By dusk it was quiet again. I turned on the light next to the qin, but I hadn't played for years and my fingers were awkward. I just listlessly moved my hand lightly across the strings. I don't know what time it was when I finally stopped. Afterwards I just sat there, gazing at the sheets of music.

Papa came in and said, "Invite a few of your friends over this evening! Tell them to come to dinner!"

I agreed, but then I remembered most of my friends had already gone away for the holidays. There was Xing, of course. She lives rather far away, in the western part of the city and whenever I invite her she always brings her younger brother and sister along. But tonight, I thought, the more the merrier!

Xing said it was late, and that if she didn't arrive on time we shouldn't delay dinner. It was already dark. In fact, this was when Xing usually left our house to go home.

Aunty and Uncle came and we were all very merry. It felt like an ordinary family evening rather than a celebration or a farewell. Uncle told tales of the sea and jokes he'd heard from sailors who'd returned from abroad.

Our kitchen is between the two courtyards and I could hear cook pacing back and forth, muttering to herself, "Nine o'clock!" She was just behind the curtain, and I could hear her quite clearly. I told Mama, "Let's go ahead and eat. Cook is wearing herself out with worry – and Xing might not be here for a while, yet." Mama protested, "But you invited her! Shouldn't we wait just a little bit longer?" As she spoke she glanced across at Papa, and their eyes met. Papa said,

"Let's start! After all, we invited Aunty and Uncle, too. We're a punctual household and whenever people are late we always end up like this!"

I knew Mama and Papa feared I wouldn't be able to eat anything, tonight. But now that Aunty and Uncle were here it was the same as if Xing was here, because everyone was happy and chatting. Surrounded by all the lively talk and laughter, I happily finished my dinner.

And a little later Xing arrived with Xian and Yi. Ji and I went out to greet them and we all came in together.

It's best to say your farewells a week or so before you go. When you are actually leaving, it's hard to know what to say. Everything is confused and you can't find the words you need to say the important things. So you stand at the station chatting meaninglessly and it all seems even more confused and hazy and you can't remember the things you meant to say.

Out of everything, I only remember a single sentence!

I was with Xing. Yi and Ji and Xian were in the next room, separated from us by a screen. We could hear them talking.

Suddenly Xing made a quick gesture with her hand. She listened for a while and then asked, "Can you hear what they're are talking about?"

"What?" I asked.

"Your little brother is saying, When my sister leaves home we are all going to feel as if we've lost a beautiful, bright jewel!" Xing giggled, and I blushed.

My brothers and I have always given high-sounding nicknames to one another! Swordsman, poet, philosopher, fairy spirit – all sorts of things. Mostly it's three parts love and seven parts joking, but sometimes it's just plain teasing. For instance, if Mama or Papa asks someone to run an errand and we all respond, the quickest to reply is the one who gets praised. So the rest of us stand there nodding and saying things like, "A worthy child! Truly filial and obedient! There are 24 legendary filial sons and you are the 25th ..." Usually, this leads to a quarrel.

But these things happen in families. And, foolish little boys sometimes say foolish things that I'd never have the nerve to utter –

So I smiled to hide my feelings.

When Aunty and Uncle left, we all moved into the middle room. It was already late. I was feeling a little upset but I went ahead and cut slices of watermelon for us.

My little brothers ran in and out, never keeping still for a moment. Xian didn't have anyone to keep him company, and he said he was tired. "We'll leave", Xing said. "We've got a long way to go. See you tomorrow, at the station!" She sounded a bit sad – little did she know that she wouldn't see me at the station, although she'd come to farewell me at the ship, two weeks from now! I was already thinking about these things.

After I saw them off, I came back into the middle room. My brothers had gone to bed. I went inside and found Papa, alone in the lamplight. I asked where Mama was, and Papa said she'd gone to bed. I could hear her moving about and coughing quietly, but I knew she didn't need me so I didn't lift the curtain.

There was silence for a while. Then Papa said thoughtfully, "When I left home I was 17 years old. Your grandfather told me, When you go out into the world just remember three words. Diligence, caution ..."

He hadn't finished, but I bowed my head and pressed

my hand against my heart – Papa looked at me, frowning. "What's wrong?"

"Nothing," I replied. "Just a little heartburn …"

Papa sighed and stood up. "It's late," he said. "Go to bed. It's already 1 AM."

I went to my room and reluctantly climbed into bed, patting the pillow. To my surprise, I slept well.

I ate breakfast alone. I told Mama I was going to the Girls' Youth Center to say goodbye to a few friends, and went out. Time seemed to be passing quickly, but also slowly. I came home just before noon.

As soon as I came through the door I felt terribly sad. My brothers blocked my way, taking photographs of me. When they finished, I went to my room and leaned against the bookshelves for support. Tears poured down my face like rain.

Aunty came in, holding little Yin. "Look!" she said. "Little Yin has come to invite her cousin to our place to eat dumplings!" I hurried over to them and caught hold of Little Yin, hugging her and smiling. One of my tears landed on her face and she ran back to Aunty.

I couldn't manage to eat much. My heart ached. I kept dipping my dumpling into the vinegar and ginger sauce again and again. Papa paced back and forth, joking with Little Yin but also paying close attention to how much I was eating. This made it even worse. My tears trickled into the bowl and I put down my chopsticks. Aunty and Sister-in-law also had tears in their eyes, but what could they do? I stood up and left without looking back …

At home, they were just clearing away lunch in the middle room. Mama was there, and when she saw me she began to cry, too. Now I was completely miserable. I feared that when people came to see me off I'd embarrass myself by crying in front of them, but even that, I thought, would be better than this.

"Mama!" I exclaimed, and sat down next to her. We gripped one another's arms with cold, quivering fingers and sobbed soundlessly – half a day of deceiving ourselves and trying to comfort ourselves, trying to deceive and comfort one another – it all came pouring out in tears and sorrowful murmurs.

The house was very quiet. Nobody came to console us. I don't think anyone could bear much more of this, either.

I let go of Mama and lay down. My tears were finished. Closing my eyes, I just lay there for a long time, feeling a great emptiness. Outside, people came and went. Mama left the room. Then a few students who had read some of my stories arrived, so I got up and washed my face and forced myself to go out and chat with them.

Someone said, "The carriage is here."

They all rushed out to fetch their bicycles, taking out handkerchiefs and clustering tearfully around me at the door.

With a tiny smile I said, "Let's go!"

The words seemed empty and the sound of my voice seemed to have come out of nowhere, entering my ears and shocking me. I lifted the curtain and went out without looking at anyone.

It all happened so fast! I turned and saw one of my brothers standing at the window, but when I looked at him he shot me a wretched glance and turned away! Poor little boy! He hadn't spoken to me since yesterday. Today, he hadn't even come out to help me keep my courage up. In that quick glance there was farewell, regret, solicitude, endless, unspoken emotion. And I completely understood. What a different person he'd become today! And all because I was leaving home. Then I remembered. Today is his birthday! I thought. And his cruel, eldest sister won't be here to eat longevity noodles with him!

Beyond the gate, I had the impression of oceans and mountains of people, as if every member of the family – young and old, high and low – had come to see me off. But I didn't see Mama. I don't know if it was because I didn't dare to look for her, or because she was hidden behind someone else, or because she simply wasn't there. I saw Aunty and Sister-in-law, both weeping. Bai and Zhang were standing at the back and called out, "Have a good trip!" But their eyes were red, and their voices were choked by sobs.

We set off, me in the carriage, the students on their bicycles. I'd invited a couple of the girls and boys to ride in the carriage with me and now the door banged shut. The horse tossed its mane and the carriage backed and turned. We made several turns, but all I could see were walls and street corners. There were so many people in the carriage with me that I couldn't see past them …

With another tiny smile, I learned back. I was in a dream! Everything that happened from now on would be part of a dream!

As I say, it was a muddled, dazed and hurried departure. Neither lingering nor tragic – yet so feared and then so regretted for so many days afterwards.

Muddled, dazed and hurried as it was, it somehow wafted me away to a cloud-like dream world! For several months it seemed to me that I was suspended in clouds and mists, and that everything skimming past before my eyes was mere illusion. All the colors, sounds, tastes, textures and odors were strange, numb and fleeting. I grappled with reality but somehow couldn't manage to grasp it!

This wasn't altogether a bad thing. During those early months I sometimes felt that it was all simply unbearable. In my distress, tossing and turning and unable to do anything, I'd look around – utterly at a loss – and then I'd say to myself, It doesn't matter. It's just a dream!

When attacks of homesickness stabbed me like knives, it was my misty, muddle-headedness that got me through!

August 4, 1923

En Route

Yesterday afternoon, I left home. When the bus turned the corner, I turned and looked back ... now, I thought, I have become a girl in a dream and I won't wake up from this dream until I'm back with the people I love, standing under our green trees!

When I left the house, I saw even more people crowded around the bus-stop. And lots of other people came to the station to see me off. I felt sad, but I felt proud, too. And deeply honored. After all, who was I to be loved so much? Who was I to deserve such a warm and moving farewell?

There were still a few minutes left before the train departed. When it was time for my little brother Bingji and the others to leave, I finally understood utter unhappiness! Little Bingji kept tugging at the others' sleeves and saying, I want to go back! I want to go back! He stood there, his eyes full of tears and finally I called him back to me, and held his face in my hands for a moment. But then my hands dropped helplessly to my sides, and my brothers left the platform -- and I hadn't managed to say even a single word!

Slowly, the train left the station. The grey walls of the city and the green willow trees flashed before my eyes. I felt very empty inside. My heart seemed dark as death. I picked up the book that I'd brought with me, and tried to read it. As soon as I turned to the first page I noticed several clumsy words scrawled in the margin: Don't forget your little brother! My heart tightened inside my chest, and I put the book down and then went and sat in another seat. It was Bingji's writing. Oh Bingji, how awful you made me feel about leaving you behind!

I couldn't sleep that night. Several times, I sat up in my bunk and looked out the window, but all I could see was a dim, half-moon shining down on dark, unlit fields. The train raced along like lightening, the wheels singing clickety-clack, carrying me towards tomorrow. The moon and I were traveling side by side, and every minute took both of us further away from home.

This morning the train passed through Jinan. I got up at five and brushed my hair, using the window-pane as a mirror. Outside, mountain ranges stretched away into the distance, so blurred and hidden by the morning mists that they were nearly invisible. For miles and miles, all I could see were pale, blue rows of mountain peaks stretched horizontally across the sky. People live in the valleys of these mountains, and the smoke from their chimneys rises up from the little villages and mingles with the clouds. Bright rays of sunshine beamed down upon the square, green fields. I washed and dressed and then just stood there looking out at the scenery for nearly half an hour. In the midst of such solemn vastness, I could only stand there in respectful silence, my head bowed before the breathtaking beauty, power and wisdom of Mother Nature.

By the time we passed Taianfu, the morning mists had lifted. We stopped at several stations, each of them nestled in deep shade. The platforms were old and beautiful and still, and I thought they looked very interesting. For the first time, I got off the train and walked around. The sight of Taishan Moutain looming in the distance made me think of other, distant things.

Now, at every stop we could hear the sound of leather boots marching along the station platforms, and the rattle of weapons clanking and crashing together. Men in yellow and grey uniforms were formed into patrols and marching back and forth. I thought all of this must have something to do with the Lincheng train robbery that I'd read about just before I left Beijing. Soon, we'd pass the very ridge where that robbery had taken place. I couldn't wait to see it! It made me think about the famous bandits and heroes in the books I read when I was little. I'm not really interested in old temples and palaces, but I love hearing about bold, wild, reckless heroes who always win through no matter how the odds are stacked against them.

At the next stop, I got off the train again. When I saw a man carrying a gun and nailing schedules on the wall, I asked him how much further it was to the ridge. He said we'd reach Lincheng soon, but that the ridge was 10 li further away and that I probably wouldn't be able to see it from the train. We chatted like old friends, both of us speaking Shandong dialect, the same dialect I speak at home. I felt very happy, just like any traveler in a distant land who suddenly hears someone speaking her native language. Shandong accents were the first sounds I heard, and I love the trustworthy people of Shandong and their shy, careful way of speaking.

Station by station, we are drawing closer to Jiangnan. I have to admit that I am beginning to enjoy the journey. Even so, I'm also looking forward to being in a proper room of my own again. A bit of freedom, a bit of quiet and a bit of news, that's what I'd really like! I'm sitting quite close to the window, and leaning against a pillow. The windows on the side of the train that faces the sun are all covered up, but the curtains on the shady side are partly open, and I'm looking out at the scenery. There's a gentle, cool wind blowing. The shaded compartment is peaceful and quiet. Except for the monotonous sound of the train's wheels, I could almost be back at home in my own little study! Of course, there are no books and book-shelves here; but there are wonderful landscapes passing by just outside the window. My pen is in my hand, and my head is full of things I want to write and so long as I don't ring the bell, nobody will come to disturb me ... I never dreamed I'd feel so peaceful and happy this morning!

Writing this letter has made me feel so much better. I hope my little brother will like it, and I hope you like it, too.

August 9, 1923
Shanghai

Well, we finally did get to Lincheng, and I did get off the train. But the only thing I saw was a group of men in uniforms, waving red flags with "Second Company" written on them and blowing horns and setting off fire-crackers. Beyond the station there were fields, and mountains, but I couldn't see anything else. I was really disappointed. I'd hoped I might at least have caught a glimpse of an armed bandit in black clothes fleeing for his life!

Now, we were traveling south and the sky was covered with clouds. Sometimes, there were little ponds beside the railroad tracks, with children splashing and playing in the shallow water at the edges. I saw a group of little girls wearing big red flowers and sitting beneath a tree, doing needlework. The sight of those little bent heads stitching away so industriously touched me, it was so beautiful.

Further south, past Xiuzhou at Bengbu, so much rainwater had collected on both sides of the railroad track that it formed a miniature lake. Tiny sailboats moved to and fro across the surface of this little lake, which was covered with ripples reflecting the sunset, making a picture so beautiful that I simply can't describe it.

It was here I noticed that people's accents were beginning to change. People in the south part of China speak quite differently from people who live in the north. And for some reason, this makes me feel slightly ill at ease -- I don't know why.

By the time we passed Nanjing, it was dusk. All I could see from the train were the lamp lights shining brightly on the far side of the Yangtze River. I'd just been thinking about Mochou Garden inside the city, but I couldn't see it. All I saw were yellow-colored waves lapping against the sides of the little boats passing directly beneath the bridge.

We passed Suzhou very early the next morning. I hadn't slept well for two nights and by now I was feeling tired and irritable. But the wonderful scenery outside my window cheered me up so much that soon I was almost dizzy with delight. Here, the river flows in dozens of rivulets among the fields. There are water-wheels in the distance, and cluster upon cluster of thatched-roofed peasant cottages. The trees are reflected in the water, which swirls itself into gentle waves beneath the graceful, hanging branches. A peasant woman carrying a hoe on her shoulder walks past. It is all as pretty as a poem or a painting.

Sometimes, caught a glimpse of the river itself. The tiny sails of the boats look particularly sharp and clear in the dawn light. I'm used to Northern landscapes, and the softness and warmth of these southern lands along the Yangze River astonishes me.

The train reaches Shanghai at seven-thirty in the morning, and once again I'm met by friends. The younger children call me "Aunty" and make me feel very welcome -- by now, I've been traveling for four or five days, but after a rest, I'm once again up and about and busy.

It's lovely and cool now, and I'm sitting here alone in the lamplight. For the past few hours, I've hardly had a moment to myself. As you know, I used to live here in Shanghai. Old friends who heard I'd be passing through have been stopping by all night, just to have a chat and to enjoy the cool, evening breezes. Three different times I've picked up my pen but as soon as I begin to write, the doorbell rings -- and there stands yet another friend who's come to see me! So of course, I have to stop writing. It goes without saying that I was happy to see my friends, but being interrupted again and again while trying to write this letter was discouraging!

That's why I've only told you a few of the things that have happened, even though there are other things that you'd find interesting. The thing is, I don't want to write a rushed, hurried letter and then have to write it all over again tomorrow. And it's very late. So I'll say good-night for now.

August 12, 1923
Shanghai

I woke up at five this morning, feeling so wide-awake and rested that I decided to take advantage of the peace and quiet to tell you about a few of other things that happened on the train.

When we stopped at Bengbu, a woman and her daughter boarded, and the conductor brought them to the compartment where I was sitting. They were carrying baskets, and one of the baskets was full of baby chickens. It was hot on the train, and the tiny chicks kept poking their heads out of the basket, trying to get a breath of air. The girl kept pushing them back in. Her movements were very quick and awkward, like a puppet on a string. This girl was dressed in trousers, and a cotton blouse, and she was about twenty years old. Although her face was covered with pockmarks, she was wearing face-powder and had decked herself out from head to toe with different pieces of jewelry. She had clasps in her hair, pearl earrings in both ears, rings on her fingers and bracelets on her arms. Whenever she spoke, she also struck a pose, just like an actress. Perhaps it was because it was so hot and the heat was making me edgy -- or perhaps there was some other reason -- but I thought she was quite disagreeable. So I looked out the window and didn't say anything to either of them. But when the girl began to speak to her mother, I couldn't resist turning around to have another look. In a very demanding tone of voice, she told her mother that she wanted soup, and some water to drink. Between you and me, she sounded like a real spoiled brat!

The mother was dressed in a blouse and trousers made of light green, gauzy stuff. She looked about fifty, and wasn't wearing any make-up. When she turned to reply to her daughter, her words were gently reproachful, but spoken lovingly. Watching them, I felt a sudden, sharp pang of sorrow. I was sure they'd look after my things if I left the compartment for a moment, and so I did -- watching them together made me think of my own mother! Not realizing my face was reflected in the glass of the corridor window, I wept a few homesick tears.

I'm not embarrassed to tell you how I felt and what I was thinking, because I know you won't laugh at me.

In fact, I'll tell you something else. Last year, when I realized I would be making this journey, I secretly started counting the number of days I had left at home. This made me so anxious that I could barely eat, and I got thinner and thinner. People saw how worried I was and tried to comfort me by saying things like, Don't take it all so seriously! This is something to be happy about, not something to dread!

Obviously, I knew that winning a scholarship to study in the United States was something to be happy about. And if it came to that, I could make myself sound cool and confident. But then I'd despise myself for pretending to be so serene when actually, I was terrified.

One day when I was visiting at Aunty's house she invited me to sit down and have tea. With a smile she inquired, "Will you miss your mother very much?"

Politely, I smiled back and said, "Really, I'm not worried about it. I won't be gone for all that long. And besides, there'll be lots of people there who'll look after me".

When Aunty left the room for a moment, my little cousin came running up to me and placed both her hands upon my knees. Staring up at me she demanded, "Cousin, is that true? You really won't miss your mama?"

When I looked into that bright, earnest little face, my eyes suddenly filled with tears. I couldn't hold them back. I felt like someone scrambling down a steep mountain and groping for a grip.

Taking my cousin's two little hands firmly in mine, I said quietly, "Of course I'll miss my mother. I'll miss her so much I don't know how I'm going to bear it. I'll miss all the people I love so much I don't know how I'm going to bear it!"

You have to admire adults. It seems so easy for them to hold back their tears. They're always so brave and so strong. Whenever I was terribly frightened or unhappy, my parents just remained calm, and comforted me. I don't know how they act behind my back, but when I'm with them they've always been understanding, tolerant and strong. I'm very grateful they're like that.

But weak as I am, I still have my pride and don't want to expose my weaknesses in public. So before I left, I always made it a point to smile and chat and be cheerful when I was with teachers or other adults, because I didn't want them to laugh at me.

Outside the window of the room where I'm sitting now, there's a slanting wind. A fine rain is falling. Would you believe that I've written all of this without stopping?

Shanghai

August 16, 1923

:   By the time you read this letter, I will have already left China. My beloved China, your borders tracing the shape of a flowering crab-apple leaf upon the map! When you read this, I'll be somewhere out in the middle of the Pacific Ocean. But I don't want to write about homesickness, because I don't want to worry you or make you sad.

So let's talk about something else. I have a suggestion. You're reading this on the "Young People's Page" ... but did you know that everything on this page used to be written by people your age?, You know what I think? I think you ought to "reach for an inch and take a yard" and try to reclaim this lost territory! If something good happens to you, write a story about it and then we can all enjoy it together. And if something awful happens, there's no harm in writing about that as well ... even if we all end up in tears.

The important thing is to relax and write honestly, without worrying about what parents or teachers might say.

To be honest, I think some of the things they talk about are so subtle and so profound that you and I haven't a hope of even understanding them. And I don't know why, but it often seems to me that what they consider right and wrong are the opposite of what we think are right and wrong. They ignore things that make us weep even to think about them. Yet things that are meaningless to us often strike them as being the most important things in the world.

Let me give you an example. Suppose there's just been a terrible battle someplace, and thousands of people have been killed and wounded, their maimed bodies lying on the ground. You and I don't have to actually see it with our own eyes. All we have to do is to hear people talking about it. Just the thought of a battle like that makes our hearts pound and gives us such awful nightmares that sometimes we can't sleep. But older people don't seem to care. In fact, they're the ones who make the battles happen in the first place.

Here's another example. You and I are Chinese, but do we care who becomes President of China? So long as whoever does become President is honest and lets us all live in peace, we'll be happy to get on with our lives. Yet the adults I know talk of nothing else! Some want this candidate and some want that one, and the struggle becomes more complicated than the most complicated game you or I could even imagine.

That's why I don't think we should worry ourselves about such things. We can't do anything about them, anyway. Adults don't really take much notice of most of what we do. Here we've got our own page in the newspaper, so let's use it to say what we like without worrying about being laughed at! So that's the end of my speech. Do I hear applause?

I'm thinking about myself again. For the next couple of months, I probably won't get any news from home, other than letters that may be waiting for me in Japan when our ship arrives there next week. Mail travels slowly over such great distances. But the autumn winds are growing colder, and it's a good time of year for writing, so I hope you'll all really make an effort!

Quite a few interesting things have happened to me here in Shanghai and I'd like to tell you about them, but I'm too busy to write any more. Once I'm actually on board ship with nothing to look at but the sea, I'll be able to take all the time I need and write everything down. So please be patient.

After tomorrow afternoon, I will really be on my way! May God protect us all, and may we all be safe, and well.

August 20, 1923
Shenhu

I just stood and watched as we set sail. All the other passengers were clutching the ends of colored paper streamers which they'd flung out of the ship's portholes. The streamers floated and fluttered towards the shore, where excited crowds of people who'd come to see us off snatched and grabbed at them. Gazing at this scene made me feel as if my spirit was soaring along with the paper streamers, towards the shore and the sky. The dozens of people on the quay all clung to the ends of the streamers as if they could hold the ship motionless. But one by one, the streamers broke and floated away on the breeze. Suddenly, this great monster -- our ship -- was free.

Shipboard life is healthy and wholesome, and there's plenty to do. Our meals are served at set times, but otherwise, we can take walks around the deck and amuse ourselves doing whatever we like. After three days of this, I became like a little child again, tying knots, tossing bean-bags and enjoying all the different games and entertainments until I wore myself out.

Later, I wondered why I'd behaved so oddly during those first three days. I think it's because being at sea made me remember things that happened when I was very young, that I'd all but forgotten. Listening to the waves, I'd find myself suddenly recalling a particular childhood game, or some childhood friends. What a shame there weren't any children on board! During those three days of my "childhood" I might have been able to play my games with them.

When I was little, we lived near the sea. But I'd never seen it looking like this, smooth and still as a mirror. The day after we left Shanghai, our ship was surrounded by tiny, clear ripples of water stretching in all directions as far as the eye could see. There was a cool breeze, and it felt as if we were gliding on ice. All the way to the horizon, the sea lay flat as a lake. The green sea and the blue sky seemed to merge together there, beneath the rays of the setting sun which reached from the distant universe across the sea to the railings of the deck. As my fascinated gaze moved from sky to water, the colors seemed to magically transform themselves from a pale, pale pink to a deep emerald green, layer upon layer of color flowing and merging into one other ... what a shame I can't draw, or paint. When it comes to describing marvelous scenes like this, I think words must be the most useless things in the world!

The following evening was the night Cowherd meets Weaving Maiden ... you all know that story, don't you? After dinner I went up on deck and just stood there by myself, leaning against the railing. The cool breeze ruffled my sleeves, and the Milky Way was a great blaze of stars shining down upon the dense, black sea. I could hear the voices of the people below-deck, talking and laughing. Suddenly, I felt very far from home. The combination of the twinkling stars and murmuring waves made me both sad and wistful.

By dusk the next day, we were nearing Shenhu, sailing through straits with green mountains on either side. Fishing boats passed to and fro. Most of these Japanese mountains looked quite round and flat to us, and everyone laughed at them and called them "Steamed Bun Mountains". We passed lots of these "Steamed Bun Mountains" before nightfall. By the time we docked at Shenhu, the decks and quays were ablaze with lamplight.

The ship came slowly to a stop, and afterwards, quite a few people went ashore. However, I thought it was too late to go sightseeing. Instead, I made my way to the highest part of the ship and there, for the first time, I was able to gaze down upon the whole ship, and upon the glittering quays and town that lay beyond. The stars and the crescent moon shone just as bright and clear as the lamps on either side. Every so often, a beam of light flashed in the mountains. I think it was probably a train. It was very still aboard the ship. Even the tide was soundless. Suddenly, I thought, If only Mama could be here with me now! And I pictured my home as clearly as if I was there! Forgive me, but now I feel so homesick that I can't bear to write another word ..

* * * * *

This morning many of us went ashore. In the distance, we could see green grass growing in the shape of an anchor on Anchor Mountain. It covered half the mountain, and was a truly beautiful shade of green.

Shenhu's main street is like the main street of a Chinese town. There are shops on both sides of the street, but the buildings are very low. All sorts of toys and books are displayed in the shop windows, and it all looks very colorful and tempting. Lots of children crowded round looking at the things in the shops. Their bright, black eyes set in small, round faces topped with thick, black hair were completely adorable.

There were several houses at the foot of the mountain, tastefully constructed with wooden walls, bamboo windows and purple flowers cascading over the tops of the courtyards. Beyond the houses, a little bridge crossed a stream. We'd planned to climb the mountain and see the twin valleys and waterfalls, but soon after we'd started up, we met some of our fellow passengers who were already coming back down. They said that our time here was almost up and we were afraid the boat might leave without us, so we went back on board.

While we were ashore, everyone went to the post office to buy stamps and post letters and the Shenhu Post Office was packed with homesick Chinese students. We've only been away for three days. How much could we possbily have to say?

After they'd returned to the ship, some students said, What's the point of trying to talk to them? We don't speak Japanese, and when we speak English, they don't understand that, either. When we write out the characters and ask, Where's the liveliest place in town? they just stare at us. Then when we ask, Where are the most beautiful gardens? they suddenly wake up and send us to the busiest part of town! They all laugh, but I don't think it's funny.

August 22, 1923
Hengbin

By dusk, we'd reached Hengbin. White clouds surrounded the setting sun, hiding its red face; I thought it looked like a Japanese lantern made out of red paper.

Standing by the railings and looking at the unbroken ridges of the mountains was very pleasant. I happened to have several empty glue tubes. Now, I stuffed them with little strips of paper, sealed them, and threw them into the sea to float away. On each strip of paper I'd written: No matter who finds this, I wish you good luck! Your countryman prays that God will bless you, Asian sailor on an Asian sea! And I also wrote: Oh, that I could ride the wind home again, for I fear these decorated jade palaces! And high places are always cold! I wrote other things, too.

Hengbin was just a transit stop, for as soon as we arrived, we boarded the Tokyo train. First, we visited the Chinese Youth Society. Then we went out to a Japanese restaurant to eat Japanese food. The restaurant was called, Heavenly Aroma. I don't remember much else about it.

When we took off our shoes to go in, we couldn't help giggling ... we aren't accustomed to that sort of thing! The waitresses were all barefoot, and we couldn't understand a word they said, so all we could do was to smile at one another. We sat on the floor, but when we looked closely at the walls and windows, we noticed that they were so smooth that they seemed to have been polished. It was cloudy outside. But inside, everything was spotlessly clean, quiet and very nicely arranged. I had a very simple meal of white rice, beef, noodles and some tea. There was a vegetable dish, but the vegetables were very tough and I only ate one mouthful.

After we'd eaten, there was a sudden downpour. We couldn't postpone our sightseeing, but it wasn't very leisurely. We sped through the rain in a bus, passing the Botanical Gardens, the National Shrine and the Zoo. We only managed to visit half a dozen places, and even then we raced in and out so quickly that they didn't leave much of an impression. You know the saying about "Looking at flowers while riding on horseback" -- well, looking at flowers in the midst of a thick mist is even worse, and looking at them as you race through the rain in a bus is worse yet! What more can I say? I also had a slight fever, so I didn't enjoy braving the rain. I wasn't really in the mood for sightseeing. Yet even so, two places stuck in my memory.

One was the Imperial Palace Bridge. This is a wonderful little bridge with white stone balustrades and the river flowing just beneath it, next to the palace walls, When I saw it, my muddled brain suddenly became clear, and I got out of the bus to take a photo. Off to one side I spotted a policeman coming towards me, and I knew he wanted to stop me from taking photos. All the same, I managed to get several shots before I got back on the bus -- unfortunately it was raining, so the photos won't come out very well. But I'll keep them, anyway.

There were mementos of the Japanese victory over China in the guest-house, and war pictures hanging on the walls. Looking at them made my blood boil with rage. Although I'm no zealot, the blood pounded in my head and I felt so dizzy that I had to sit down. Some of the others murmured angrily at the sight of these things, but I didn't say a word.

I'm sorry to be telling you about this, for despite my "warrior's heart", I often feel a fondness for individual Japanese, rather than humiliation and hostility. It's not the Japanese people who are to blame, but the Japanese government. Even so, I can't bear hearing about how they rode roughshod over other human beings!

I love my brother, because we're the same flesh and blood. If I had cake and he asked for some, I'd smile and give it to him. But if he used brute strength to wrest the cake away from me, I'd have no choice but to fight back and defend myself. And it would be even worse if he was doing this to me because some Government told him to do it! Despite the love in my heart, I would have to resist, even if it meant destroying the cake rather than letting him have it.

33

Forgive me for going on like this. But think about what I've written, too.

We took the 5 PM train back to Hengbin, and came aboard.

August 23, 1923
At sea

I've had a fever, and it's cloudy and raining. I'm not feeling very well today. Most of the other passengers have gone ashore, and I'm sitting by myself "standing guard" over the ship. Sitting here alone on the deck, I find myself thinking about yesterday at the railway station, and all the different sounds the wooden clogs made upon the pavements. Then I remember the day before yesterday during a service on the ship, when they sang "God Protect My Mother" and how upset it made me. Then the sun came out, and I could hear a hubbub of voices and see all the traders and vendors below on the quay, the noise and confusion making me giddy.

The other passengers returned, and that afternoon, we set sail. Soon we could no longer see land, and I thought, We will not see land again until the end of our voyage, when everything will be completely different.

I'd written a letter for you and wanted to post it before we sailed, but by the time I rushed out of my cabin and up on deck, the ship was already moving gently away from the shore. Knowing it would be at least ten days before I could post it, I threw it into the sea.

That night, I dreamed that Mama was here, touching my forehead and saying: You're very hot -- take nine spoonfuls of your medicine. She was holding a cup of medicine, and she told me to drink it up. The medicine was yellow-colored, and I swallowed it in a single gulp. In the dream, it tasted like orange juice. When I woke up all I could hear were the sounds of the wind and the sea beyond the porthole. So I turned over and went back to sleep and today, my fever is gone.

"There will be wind and waves, for this is a voyage that is rarely smooth!"

I don't know when these words were written, or by which poet, but they spread instantly among the hundreds of students. None of us could remember actually hearing the line, but we all kept repeating it to one another as if we were passing along good news. In our strange and lively state of mind, we seemed to be saying it so as to guard against it, rather than because we hoped it would happen.

As for me, I chattered away more happily than ever and smiled and smiled for no reason at all.

At dusk, the lamps were lit as usual. In the vast hall, the colors of our bright clothing were reflected in the full cups. In the midst of our laughter and chatter, white-garbed waiters holding trays upon their upturned palms made their way between the circular tables … and suddenly, the sea grew rough! Everyone froze for a moment, knives and forks poised in the air. We looked at one another and smiled and rolled our eyes as if to say, There will be wind and waves – and then we could all feel the ship swaying from left to right.

I smiled with satisfaction, but I didn't say anything.

After the meal I went back to my cabin. There was a Conversation Club meeting later that evening. As I slowly changed clothes, gazing into the mirror and humming to myself, I saw my own pleasantly surprised expression in the mirror. I looked as if I was preparing to attend a mermaid's party at the bottom of the sea, or as if I was sharpening a sword in preparation for a duel with a famous master whom I was certain of vanquishing.

It was late when I went back down, as I'd took time to arrange all my things neatly upon my bed.

As I walked through the door with a pleased expression on my face, I saw several of the other girls sitting on the big soft, smiling and chatting quietly in the lamplight. Their happy voices already held a sort of giddiness.

On the way down, I'd encountered a number of my fellow passengers also coming down but carrying blankets in their arms. Their cheerful voices had also sounded a bit giddy.

Still smiling, I went out on deck. A group of people were sitting and standing in a circle near someone who was playing a stringed instrument. Fetching a chair I sat down next to Ling, who leaned against my shoulder and grinned and said, "The wind and waves have arrived!"

The person playing the stringed instrument was swaying from side to side and plucking at the strings with the fingers of both hands. The people who were singing were smiling and touching the instrument as they sang. Then suddenly the whole row of bodies involuntarily slid across the deck to the other side.

Everyone laughed, but their laughter seemed to suggest they didn't think they wanted to put up with much more of this. Gradually, they all wandered away.

I went back into the Common Room. The other members of the Conversation Club had already come in and everyone was sitting in a circle. The room seemed very stuffy. I thought some of the faces looked a little bit vacant and I noticed people were covering their mouths and sitting in cramped positions -- we were all really feeling it as the room tilted from one side to the other.

Everybody was making a great effort, but our minds were focused upon the heaving sea! As if I'd just been speaking about my love of the sea someone asked, "Why DO you love the sea? How CAN you love the sea?"

Little by little, I was starting to feel better. I gave a contented smile. I don't mean that I was pleased about the situation, but I was feeling something in my own body and soul that was coming directly from the sea. So I said, "Loving the sea means loving all of it ..."

But before I could finish my sentence one of our fellow students suddenly turned and left the room with her hand clapped over her mouth.

Everyone laughed, but there was something in their laughter that seemed to say, We're leaving, too! But then they didn't have the heart to actually go, so we went back to chatting in fits and starts. My own spirits were soaring, as if the hour of the banquet set in that mermaid's palace was drawing closer and closer; as if my dueling opponent was even now coming toward me, step by step, holding his sword – but of course, I'm just quoting "literary" phrases!

Another student turned away, put his hand over his

mouth and fled — two more of them, then three more …

I knew I ought to say something so I joked, "We're adjourned! Never mind me!" — and I stood up and left the group.

Laughing, everyone else left too. Beneath the light from the lamps, there was nobody at all on the outer deck. All you could hear were the billowing waves beyond the railings. Everyone on the ship had gone below. Smiling, I made my way to the topmost deck.

Amidst the tumult and mist, I faced into the sea breeze which swept across my forehead and ruffled my hair. Going to the railing, I took down a life buoy and sat down on it, hugging my knees to my chest and gazing up at the distant, towering perpendicular lines of the mast and the funnel. I watched the railings at the stern of the ship as they rose and fell against the horizontal line of dull, grey sky at the horizon — sometimes, by as much as five or six feet!

Concentrating as hard as I could, I listened to the roar of the sea. Looking up past the tip of the mast into the sky beyond, I saw two big stars — I was exhilarated and also serene, filled with a solemn happiness. Mother Sea, I thought, gently rocking this cradle upon the huge waves. And of all the hundreds of infants in the cradle, perhaps I am the only one who is still awake …

I thought about Mama. I thought about Papa. I remember the way Papa smiled at me just before I left and said, Don't be troubled by seasickness during the magical journey across the Pacific Ocean, my daughter!

Later, I wrote these sentences in a letter I sent to Papa: I've had a taste of the wind and the waves. I'm in the midst of the weather, sitting on the highest deck of the ship in the middle of the night just because I wanted to tell you about it. The sea has already proved that I am certainly my father's daughter.

But was this really so important? Right now the sea is like a mirror. Gentle winds blow every day, although at night we can still feel the vibrations as the hull rises and falls. The poetic exaggeration of wind and waves that we anticipated with such uneasy smiles was much greater than the reality.

August 24, 1923
At Sea

We live on the boat as if on an island surrounded by the sea. The days dissolve into one another. It's like being in a trance. As I can't remember the events of each separate day, this will be a rather sketchy account.

Among the passengers traveling in second and third class, there are a few who can play musical instruments. So every evening I sit on the top deck and listen to the music coming from below. Amidst the sounds of the waves, the tunes seem lonely and sad, and the musical notes sound like sobs. These passengers have also left their homes and their native land, and even though we don't speak the same language or think the same thoughts, in this cold, beautiful music our feelings intermingle and a deep current of love flows between us.

One night when the moon is full I linger, listening to the music and not wanting to go back down to my cabin. So I remain there on the deck, a rug draped over my shoulders to ward off the sea winds. The boat moves forward, riding the wind and cleaving the waves, towards an unknown, alien land.

The plaintive music seems to be asking: Why is this vast ship working so hard to carry all these people away from their homelands? Who are these travelers? What are their names? What do they seek?

Silently, I shake my head. If it weren't for the laughing, chattering voices coming from the upper decks and breaking into my sad thoughts, I think I might have stayed there, all by myself, until dawn.

One of our fellow passengers has brought along food and fruit, which he gives to the children traveling in second and third class. We Chinese students persuade some of the other passengers to donate things, which we collect and take down to the lower decks. There are quite a few children, and many women playing with babies on their laps. They are so adorable! But one afternoon, something happens which makes me sad, and also angry. One of the children -- who can't have even been two years old -- was particularly tiny, delicate, and alert. At first, I couldn't coax him to come to me, but when I offered him candy and showed him toys he finally came and sat on my lap. After a while, I put him down and walked away, but he came toddling after me, and clutched my knees. We were just standing there, laughing and playing, when I looked up and saw his father standing just inside the door. Although the man must have been middle-aged, you could see from his grey hair and the wrinkles and lines on his face that he'd had a difficult, unlucky life. He looked at least 60. As he gazed at his little son, his kindly, sympathetic eyes seemed to fill with tears. You know, tears of love like that are the most sacred things in the world! I believe there is nothing undignified or dishonorable about sparkling, tear-filled eyes. The tears of a young girl or a little child; tears of grief or indignation; the tears of a woman, or an old man; kindly tears, sympathetic tears; lustrous, transparent liquid pearls about to fall, gleaming with an awe-inspiring light --- I have the utmost respect for such tears, and whenever I see them, I bow my head with respect.

And this was no exception. I bowed my head, gave the child a little pat and walked away. Suddenly, the First Class Nursing Sister -- who takes care of the people who get seasick -- appeared in the doorway. Her stern gaze fell upon the toddler.

"Who let you come up to the First Class Deck? Go away, shoo! Quickly!"

The poor old man moved forward with small, hesitant steps. With a calm look and a slow, stiff smile, he picked up the child, and shot the Nursing Sister an apologetic, humiliated glance. Then, carrying the child in his arms, he moved slowly and wearily back down the steps.

Who let him come up? What a question! This loving father who was unwilling to hand his child over to a stranger had only come up here to keep an eye on his baby! I was the one who'd brought the child up here, but I hadn't thought about the father. I felt so outraged! I stared at that big, fat Nursing Sister with a really angry look on my face until she finally gave a guilty little smirk. There were quite a few people nearby, but none of them seemed to care about what had just occurred. I turned and went to my room. But that night at dinner, I had quite a few things to say!

We Chinese students organized two entertainment nights, and both times we asked the people in charge of the ship if we could invite the second and third class passengers to come up and listen to the music with us. The answer was always no. Our motives were quite straightforward and uncomplicated and it hadn't occurred to us that money might be a barrier ... so things didn't turn out as we hoped. We do our best, but we're still a long way from making this a perfect world!

The ship's attendants all come from South China, and most of the First Class passengers are young Chinese students. The attendants care quite a lot about what we think of them. A few days before we reached Seattle, they published an essay in the ship's newspaper, urging us to work hard and be a credit to China. The essay wasn't particularly elegant, but it was heartfelt and sincere. I only remember a little bit of it, about "men from the south of China crossing a foreign sea" – but the gist of it was that we shouldn't allow ourselves to simply be driven by winds and currents, nor to be underestimated by Westerners. We Chinese students wrote a sincere and respectful reply, which was also published in the ship's newspaper.

Crossing the ocean, there's nothing much to see. Watching the sunset is interesting, but it is difficult to describe with words. I did see flying fish, with locust-like wings growing out of their backs. And I also saw two big whales -- not their bodies, but their waterspouts -- in the distance.

Otherwise, shipboard life was a lot like attending a students' association meeting, with members coming and going, although never leaving the ship. Except for a few entertainments, performances and talks, we passed the long days chatting with one another and writing letters.

When you cross Pacific Ocean, an extra day suddenly appears out of thin air! We had two August 28ths! Afterwards, we were a day behind China. So now when I dream of my family at night, everyone is actually bustling about in broad daylight! Oh, you people I've left behind! I visit you every night in my dreams, but will we ever actually meet again?

We'd finished our wine and were in Papa's study. Papa was reading and I was sitting beside the books. I'd been silent for some time –

I stood up, putting both hands to my face and leaning against the table. "Papa!" I exclaimed. Papa looked up. "I've decided I'll be a lighthouse keeper!"

"Fine!" Papa smiled. "A lighthouse keeper keeps watch over the sea month after month out, year in and year out – but it's rather cold, and lonely."

Having said this, Papa went back to his book.

"I'm not afraid of being cold or lonely", I said. "I'm not, really!"

Papa put down his book. "Really? Really and truly?"

Now there was no way I could back down. Shrugging my shoulders I said, "Lighthouses are big and tall. I think it would be a very poetic way of life."

"Yes, of course." Papa nodded, and then he leaned back in his chair and settled himself as if he was about to make a long speech.

I was still standing there. "I only want to help people," I said. "I'm not just thinking of myself without considering others. I know we mustn't avoid the world, but we also mustn't make the mistake of avoiding solitude, either."

Papa smiled, and nodded again.

"Avoiding the world and leaving home are two things that I really don't want to do," I continued. "But what's the use of being young and strong if I have to sacrifice myself because my parents don't want to part with me?"

Papa just kept smiling.

"They call lighthouse keepers Givers of Light," I said bravely. "The lighthouse keeper leaves his fields, his family and every kind of amusement and activity to spend every month of the year looking at the endless sky and sea. Except for sea gulls and the sails he sees upon the sea and the windblown clouds up in the sky, he never sees anything new. In fact, if it weren't for the gusty sea breezes and the little blades of grass turning green on the steep slopes of his island, he wouldn't even know when spring arrived. I'd be leaving the so-called happy masses behind and all I'd have would be my work ..."

Papa interrupted, then.

"If what you're saying is that it's a sacrifice to separate yourself from everyone else in the world, then it's a description that also fits sailors like me."

He sighed.

"No!" I protested. "I'm not saying it would be a sacrifice! It would be an honor. Each evening, when I lifted my torch and climbed the steps, I'd feel courageous and honored. Think of all the brave men who leave home without even a farewell and must face waves and tides and fickle sea breezes, forcing the sails and the mast to do their bidding ... aren't they still part of the world? They have to endure raging winds and dense fogs and mountainous seas, and all they can do is frown, lower their heads, hold their breath and concentrate upon a beam of distant, suspended, glimmering light! To those men, that beam of light means vigilance, comfort and guidance and that beam of light is shining thanks to me!"

As if he'd suddenly remembered something, Papa gazed at me.

I went on with what I was saying. "On clear, fine days when the sea is flat and calm, I'd sit on the sand, hugging my knees and watching the falling tide and twinkling stars. On windy, rainy days I'd lean against the window, looking at the billowing waves and listening to the roaring sound of the water crashing against the rocky cliffs. I'd close all the doors and read. I'd make the sea my teacher, and I'd make friends with the moon and the stars. It would be eternal, unchanging. And every few days a little boat would arrive, bringing me news of the outside world and letters from my friends and family. Like short separations, parting never to meet again creates a certain kind of friendliness! I'd be able to read a whole book all the way through without stopping.

I'd be able to write. As far as culture is concerned, I wouldn't be separated from the world at all!"

"I've no doubt that life in a lighthouse is unconventional", Papa said. "But your imaginary picture is a bit too perfect. Suppose you fell ill, there in your lighthouse between the sea and the sky? What would you do then?"

"That's easy!" I replied. "I'd be so busy I wouldn't have time to worry about it"!

"Sickness is just a matter of your own body," Papa said. "But if you made a mistake lighting the beacon it would affect many others."

"But that's exactly why I'm saying it would be a fine and noble way of life."

My words made him smile. "I know you could climb the steps and light the beacon," he said. "But what if there were strong winds and thick fog, and a ship hit the rocks and was sinking and you had to fire the cannon and launch a boat ..."

"I'd like that best of all!" I cried passionately. "I'd be willing to learn how to do everything, for myself and for everyone else."

Papa didn't say anything for a few moments. Then he murmured, "If you were a boy you'd be my favorite son!"

"Suppose I really wanted to do this kind of work along the southeast coast?" I took a step closer to him. "Could you arrange it for me, Papa?"

"Perhaps. But why are you so set on this?"

"I've been planning it for three years," I told him solemnly.

Papa's expression became serious. Deep in thought, he rubbed at the corners of his book. "I don't disapprove," he said at last. "And I probably could arrange it. And I'm also brave enough to risk allowing my only daughter to leave home and go abroad to breathe the salt air and live the life of a sailor on the high seas, even to tend the light on some steep island. The problem is that girls aren't allowed in lighthouses!"

I managed a stiff little smile, and went back to where I'd been sitting.

There was rather a long silence.

Papa stood up. "A noble, bright and brilliant life can be lived in other places besides a lighthouse," he said, trying to comfort me. "The world is a big place!"

I didn't reply. I sat there for a while longer and then lifted the curtain and went into the other room.

My little brothers were standing in a corner, lighting firecrackers and throwing them at one another and laughing happily. A couple of the firecrackers accidentally landed near me but I just good-naturedly dodged them – I really wasn't in the mood to play.

I went to my room and listlessly lay down on my bed in the dark. Even if my New Years dream wasn't going to come true, dreaming it was better than nothing. I wanted to go back into my dream, so in my imagination I created a scene with dark billowing waves and a towering white lighthouse …

There was only darkness, and silence. I couldn't even make myself dream my dream!

All of that took place two years ago. I didn't brood about it. In fact, if I hadn't seen a lighthouse I'd probably never have even thought about it again.

But during the past few weeks at sea, I've caught glimpses of several lighthouses. And each time, I heave a sad little sigh. I never again wanted to feel the way I felt that night. But tonight, in the thick mist, I become quite sorrowful.

There is a fine drizzle. I climb to the top deck. Leaning on the railing I suddenly see – beneath the canopy of the heavens and in the midst of the enveloping fog – two mountain peaks. They emerge from the blackness and became two islands, each with its own, star-like twinkling light –––

The ship is rocking slightly from left to right. The two points of light also gently rise and fall from side to side. The beams of light penetrating the layers of fog send a lustrous, bright shining sensation straight into my soul. It is like a greeting, like guidance. I am silent for a long time, and my sorrow abates.

So many useless, regretful tears were wiped away that night, thanks to those two points of light! I can thank the roaring sea for carrying my old, secret wishes back to me in the beams of light from two lighthouses –

And so it was settled. As I'd taken it up, I now put it down. No longer did I yearn to be a lighthouse keeper. Nor would I ever again dream about lighthouses. Where there's no hope, there's no disappointment. Not wanting something and knowing that you'll never be able to want it means that you'll never be miserable about not having it.

God bless whoever lit those two, bright lights! God bless all the lighthouse keepers around all the edges of the sea! May their seas always be calm, may their steep little islands always be green. I hope they know they are kings without crowns. I admire them so much.

September 1, 1923

Early this morning, we reached Victoria. Once again, we could see land. But my impressions were so confused! The sun blazed magnificently down upon the sea, flocks of gulls flew overhead, and little boats swept towards us upon green waves that lapped at the sides of the little islands all around. That first night, I was so distracted by the sound of the wind blowing in off the sea that I didn't sleep well. The next morning, photographers came on board and we all had to sit in the sun to have our group photograph taken. There were flags flying, and they played the national anthem over and over again for what felt like half the day. When we finally did go ashore, we were mostly kept busy with all the official things that needed to be done.

Then we floated gently into Seattle. There were a number of golden-haired people on the quay, hurrying back and forth and climbing onto the ship … it made for a strange scene! Hurriedly, we disembarked. With one hand resting on the railing, I turned and looked back at our ship, silently anchored alongside the shore. Suddenly, I felt depressed. Our journey across the sea was over and now we were about to become aimless, wind-driven bits of duckweed, scattering to our separate destinations.

The city of Seattle is set amidst three mountains and two lakes. Streets and thoroughfares link it from one end to the other. The country is hilly and undulating, but very attractive. Fifty years ago, all of this was wilderness. But now it's completely built up and so beautifully maintained that one realizes what a vigorous nation this is.

I took part in a hurried tour of the lakes and mountains, attended several welcoming receptions, and on the 3rd, boarded the train to Chicago. This was a special train for Chinese students, so everyone spoke Chinese, although the dialects came from all over China.

September 3, 1923

The most interesting part of the train journey was when we passed through the Rocky Mountains, which took a whole day. As we slowly wound our way through the peaks, the train resembled a long snake surrounded on all sides by lofty, tumbling mountains. There was an Observation Car at the back, where we could sit and look out at the scenery. Those great, green mountains and rocky outcrops everywhere made us aware of how small and insignificant we were! But you know, I've never though looking at mountains is as pleasant as looking at water. In fact, it can be very gloomy.

There's nothing else worth telling about the trip. We passed station after station as swiftly as the wind, and none of it left much of an impression, although when we crossed the bridge over the Mississippi River beneath a new moon, the scenery was exquisite. That was a wonderful sight.

We arrived in Chicago on the morning of the seventh day. A bus met us at the station and we were immediately taken off to see the sights. It was a wet, cloudy day, and I was very conscious of the smell of petrol in the busy streets. Despite the dull weather it was all very lively, and we saw Negroes everywhere. We visited several public parks and conservatories, all of which were green, elegant and quite welcoming. I was surprised at how different Chicago was from Seattle. They have many more green, grassy spaces here than we have in Beijing.

That night, we stayed at a Youth Hostel. It rained, and falling leaves struck the windowpanes. In a letter home I wrote: *The falling leaves tell me that here in Chicago, it is autumn! Tonight we saw a film, and when the lights came on and we all stood up to leave, for a moment, I felt as if I was going home, too -- then with a shock, I realized that my home was far away on the other side of the Pacific Ocean.*

The next morning, we boarded a train for Boston. This time, I did feel alone in the crowd. There were two other Chinese students, but all the other passengers were Americans.

Once again, we raced past station after station. Now, there were flat plains outside the windows, and sometimes we glimpsed waterfalls between the rocks and trees, tumbling down the sides of distant mountains.

We reached Springfield the next afternoon, where the other two Chinese students shook hands with me and left the train. So by the time my journey from the western shore of the Pacific Ocean to the western shore of the Atlantic Ocean was done, I was the only traveler left.

September 9, 1923

At last, I was in Boston, the so-called Cultural Capital of America., After weeks of traveling, I could finally have a few days' rest.

Before I began my studies at Wellesley College, I spent three days sightseeing. I went to Greenfield, Springfield and other places, visiting men's and women's colleges like Holyoke and Smith (both women's colleges) Amherst and others. But all the students were still on vacation, so I didn't really see much except for a lot of big, college buildings.

During my sightseeing tour, I couldn't help but admire America's dense forests and smooth, flat roads.

Massachusetts has many lakes, and I especially enjoyed driving around and visiting them. At each lake the bright water was set off by the dark shade of the trees that surrounded it, and all of the lakes were very beautiful. One day we went to an Atlantic Ocean beach to watch children playing on the sand, and sea-gulls. That night, I dreamed I was a child again.

There were certainly no sandy beaches to be seen where I boarded the ship in Shanghai. Even after we'd crossed the sea and dropped anchor in Seattle, I hadn't see any beach like this one. But although it was a great novelty,

I must admit that what I remember most vividly are the endlessly rolling, crashing waves, which -- to tell the truth -- made me feel a bit uneasy.

September 17, 1923
Beside Lake Waban
Wellesley College

I've begun my academic life as an overseas student. I've only been here for a few days, and Waban Lake -- and all my other new surroundings and the deep silences -- often make me feel homesick. Even so, everything that's happened to me recently strikes me as being very exotic.

As luck would have it, I've been assigned to a room in Beebe Hall, which has associations with the sea. The building was donated to the college by Captain John Beebe, and that's why there are so many seascapes hanging in the main hall, in the rooms and in the corridors. When I first arrived, it was much too soon for letters from home to have reached me. But each time I went up or down the stairs, I stopped and stood in front of the mail table, imagining it heaped with letters. At such moments, I'd comfort myself by gazing at the enormous waves rolling through the paintings on the wall.

College is like a botanical garden, with every student representing a different kind of flower. American coeds wear makeup and are much more glamorous than Chinese girls. They wear gay, dazzling clothes, which seem quite unusual to me. They are also very vivacious and lively, but their friendships are superficial, what we'd call "Western friendships".

The morning sun is shining. Even while I'm still making my way over the grassy slopes and through the dense woodlands, I can feel the breeze from the lake. Now, sitting quietly beside the lake and surrounded by autumn leaves and the lapping sounds of the water, I'm putting pen to paper and writing to the friends I left behind in China so many months ago. Can you imagine how I feel?

The sunlight shimmers in silvery slivers upon the surface of the water. On the opposite shore, foreign flowers and row upon row of tall pine trees make it very clear to me that I am truly far from home

I don't know whether the sounds I hear are the little waves breaking against the shore or the layers of pebbles washing at the water's edge. But there's a tiny voice clamoring at my knee as if it wants to be introduced to you ... how can I possibly describe it? I've seen how lovely the lake looks beneath the setting sun, under the full moon, and even covered with thick mists and rain squalls. It's very beautiful. You could even say it's magnificent. But nobody I love is here. There is only this tiny voice -- this "lake fairy" -- to comfort me.

In English, it's called Lake Waban. But the word "Waban" sounds almost like two Chinese words that mean "comfort Bing Xin" and that's how I think of it. Each day at dusk, the little boats on the lake look like feathers, the water too soft to resist them. All the green, red, yellow and white leaves that grow on the trees surrounding the lake are reflected in the water, covering half the lake with gentle, beautifully limpid autumn colors. It's especially lovely when the sun is setting and the golden rays of late afternoon sunshine pierce the treetops and scatter themselves across the surface. Surrounded in a golden haze, I try to send my love to you upon the rays of the setting sun,

I've spent weeks at sea, and now, weeks beside this lake. But if you ask me which I like best, I can't tell you. The sea was like a mother, but the lake is like a friend. When I was small, I wanted to be near the sea. Now, I want to be near the lake. The sea is as boundless, like a mother's love for her child. It makes me feel respectful, and reverent. On the other hand, with its colorful reds and greens and blues, the lake is as warm and charming as the idle conversations one has with good friends ... is this too abstract? I hope not, because I can't think of any other way to describe it.

I hope you've written to me, and I hope you've included lots of news from home. Please consider this little note as a sort of preface. I promise that from now on, I'll write very good letters and remember to post them in order, with all of the dates and place-names just as they should be. .

It's strange, but I don't know when you'll actually receive this letter. The world is truly so very large!

October 24 1923

Wellesley College

My Dear Brothers,

   The autumn rain falls day after day here in Boston, as if it'll never stop. Red and yellow-colored fallen leaves accumulate in little piles upon the footpaths. In some places, they're several inches deep, and very soft and wet underfoot. I don't go walking to the lake quite so often now, but I still manage to go once a day, making my lonely way down the long, silent path and listening to the raindrops pattering down upon my umbrella. Smiling to myself, I wonder what I'm doing out here, walking all by myself in the rain and the wind! And when I reach the lake, all the places I used to sit -- under the trees, or upon the rocky outcrops -- are soaking wet. So I just stand there, staring into the mist. The water is pale and white, and it's impossible to see the trees at the other side of the lake, or even to see all of the lake itself. This gives it a certain air of mystery.

   By the time I've returned to my room, it's already evening. So I draw the green curtains, and turn on the lights, and read Chinese poetry. When I look at the newspapers I've just received from China, and see pictures of familiar places, I actually manage to forget that I'm here and not back home in China. Someone knocks at my door, and I call out, Qing lai! Then I look up and see a blonde, blue-eyed girl smiling at me in the lamplight, and I'm so startled that I laugh ... or sigh.

What's the latest news from Beijing, and China? Why do you suppose that I never worried about such things when I was actually living there? -- A few days ago I read a poem by an English poet named Wordsworth. The poem is carved on a stone tablet by the lake. It goes:

> I traveled among unknown men,
> In lands beyond the sea,
> Nor England! did I known 'til then,
> What love I bore to thee."

When I read these words I feel that for a fleeting moment I understand the poet's own feelings of homesickness, even though I don't really know very much about him. But as I return from the lake, neither the sight of the lamp-lit windows in the tall buildings nor the splendor of the thousands of twinkling stars in the sky can comfort me.

If I close my eyes, I can almost hear the voices of the grape-peddlers and date-sellers as they roam the Beijing streets! At home, I used to hate hearing the sound of their sad, mournful voices in the autumn wind... especially during late afternoons. I remember one Sunday afternoon when you'd all gone out boating and I was at home alone, sitting on the verandah and feeling desolate and listless. The autumn wind penetrated my clothes and the repeated cries of the date-sellers from beyond the courtyard wall penetrated my ears. I don't know why, but it made me feel terribly lonely. Then I heard your laughing, clamoring voices outside the wall and all my sad feelings evaporated. That's when I understood how much happiness and comfort a family can give; and that so long as spring breezes blow in my heart, even the harshest autumn winds can not make me unhappy. I didn't share those thoughts with you then, but I happened to think of them today. That's probably because even though there are no grape-peddlers or date-sellers crying their wares here, there is rain and wind outside the window. -- Parting is part of life. Yet parting is unbearable. What can anyone say to make me feel better?

Twice in a single day, I take my little key and, feeling both hopeful and apprehensive, go downstairs to the bank of letter-boxes. Even though I can't see the shape of an envelope through the glass door of my box, I open it anyway and look more closely. But there truly isn't anything there. Feeling very low, I go back upstairs ... twice in one day! I know that a person who is 10,000 *li* from home can't expect to get a letter every day, but I can't help looking and hoping ...really, do you blame me?

The evenings grow longer and longer. Long evenings are a good time for reading books. I wish I could somehow span the distance that lies between us and be there with you, helping you with your homework after dinner. But now that I think of it, as I sit here in the lamplight, you're probably still in your classrooms – oh! to be back home, with Mama! Those hours were precious as gold, and when you think about how much I -- here in a strange land -- envy you, perhaps you won't take them so much for granted! When I lived at home I always felt I must read and write for a certain number of hours every night, until Papa or Mama came in to tell me that it was time to stop. Then, I'd happily put pen and books aside! Now, when it grows late and everybody is tired, I simply tidy up my things all by myself and dream of coming home again. Imagine how this feels, and enjoy your happy lives.

Chrysanthemums are on the market by now, and I imagine Papa is busy ... how many is he planting this year? I've got some narcissus bulbs on my desk, and although they haven't flowered yet, they've all got buds and they look promising, which makes me happy.

It's almost time for dinner, now. American girls love dressing up, especially in the evening. As soon as the first bell rings, they busily begin dressing and powdering their faces and putting on their evening makeup. Every night, I sit at a table surrounded by beautiful young women.

I haven't really got anything more to say. But take care of yourselves, and look after one another!

I've never felt like this before. This feeling only came tonight – and calling it a feeling is not the same as calling it a shooting or a stabbing – all the same, I hope I never, ever experience anything like this again.

On the evening of August 14th after dinner, I came upstairs with a friend. As we passed the tower window, she cried out with delight and urged me to look at the moon. I opened the curtain and saw a bight, full moon suspended high in the sky over a distant tower. Moonlight flowed like quicksilver upon the ground. It was as if a whip had lashed my heart. I was suddenly, terribly homesick. I managed to say something rather confused and disjointed about how beautiful the moon was, but then I went to my room, drew the curtains shut and went to bed.

I was up early the next morning. While I was brushing my hair I suddenly remembered how disappointed and sad I'd felt the night before. Some lines of poetry came into my head:

"If I had a silver pheasant I'd set it free
I'd open the cage at dawn and set my silver
pheasant free"

If I had a silver pheasant I'd set it free, too. Last night I would have certainly opened the cage and let it go. But even though it had two wings and was able to fly, what living thing can fly all the way across the vast, Pacific Ocean? Even if I was a silver pheasant, I'd still be utterly helpless!

The day (which happened to be the day we Chinese celebrate our Mid-Autumn Festival) dawned fine and clear. Laughing heartily, E told me that tonight we'd all go out rowing on the lake. That really depressed me. I didn't want to go. But it is a tradition here that every year on this night, the old girls invite the new girls to come rowing and admire the moon ... so what could I say?

By the time they came to fetch me at dusk, the sky was completely overcast. I went along, hiding my secret feeling of gratitude that the clouds would hide the moon.

There were seven of us, in three little boats. A shove

of the punt-pole and we floated slowly under the bridge and out onto the lake. The glistening water was all around us, and the dark green colors of the surrounding mountains reflected in the emerald green water made me feel quite melancholy. Beneath the surface of the water I could see black, floating masses. There were red traces of the autumn leaves on the shore and in further away, several high buildings seemed to rotate past as the boat turned.

We drifted to the center of the lake and changed course, entering a low place where the branches hung down to the water. Chatting idly, we continually looked up at the opaque, cloudy sky. Dense clouds hid everything. There wasn't even a trace of the moon. I thought of another bit of poetry:

"They can't buy this hidden sight, not even for a thousand pieces of gold"

But of course I didn't say anything that would indicate how glad I was that we couldn't see the moon.

With the clouds hiding everything and no sign of the moon, the darkness gradually grew threatening, muffling even the brightness of the lake. Several black clouds dragged themselves across the trees at the eastern side of the lake and everyone listlessly agreed. It's hopeless! Let's go back.

On the way back the girl sitting in the stern of our boat said sarcastically, The moon! How uninspiring! But she gave me a quick smile and I smiled back at her – did she know what I was really thinking?

After we reached shore a few of the girls remained on the bank, still looking up – and I thought, What a shame!

This Mid-Autumn night has unexpectedly eluded us! Listlessly, we all made our way back, although I still didn't say anything about feeling relieved that I hadn't been forced to look at the moon.

On the 16th the evening sky was even more overcast. I became calm, even serene. I forgot about the moon.

But then I happened to knock at the door of a friend who lived on the eastern side of the building. She'd just turned off her lamp and was sitting by the window, and her room was filled with moonlight! Startled, I wanted to back away, but I couldn't. I had to stand there as she stood up and clasped my hands and drew me to the window.

And there it was! The full moon, round and bright, just as I remembered it from home. I couldn't speak. I had to bite my lip to keep from crying.

If my friend knew how dreadfully homesick I felt at that moment she certainly would not have put her arm around my waist and forced me to stand there at the window. I was silent and miserable as I tried to think of something to say that would sound appreciative. It was like standing at the edge of an abyss and looking down into an endless sea of acid. Better to simply jump than to hesitate like a ghost, palpitating with terror! Better to end this awful suffering once and for all.

Trembling inside, I struggled to control myself, to concentrate. The nearby buildings, the distant observatory, the various trees all around, the colors. Red, blue and yellow. Beneath the domes of three, green glass hemispheres perched on needle-thin poles that looked like long fingers, round, white bulbs cast circle after circle of moon-shaped light upon the ground, clear as an ink-brush painting. At the four corners where the roads crossed the green grass looked like green velvet. It never had such sharp contours by daylight, nor was there this feeling of everything being saturated by a vast, milky glow

I did start to cry, very quietly.

Homesickness had paralyzed me. When I touched my hair, I touched homesickness. When I pressed my fingertips together, all I could feel was homesickness. And I felt this homesickness throughout my whole body, as a physical sickness and not as some abstract, floating, spiritual sorrow!

Turning slowly away, I said goodbye to my friend and went back to my own room. Slowly, I covered the silver-framed photographs of Mama and Papa that sit upon my desk with a handkerchief. Slowly, I picked up a very thick book and with my head resting on my hand, tried to read it. I turned several pages but my mind was a blank and I didn't even have the strength to go through the motions of reading. So I closed the book, crept into bed and sobbed.

I really was sick …

The terror and the emotion I felt that night was like an urgent message flashing and surging into the deepest depths of my being. Just remembering it leaves me speechless, gasping with amazement! Since then, I've struggled to control my homesickness and am no longer overcome by such violent emotions. A number of other moonlit nights have come and gone and I'm sometimes awake until dawn, but I never feel anything worse than a mild wistfulness.

Sorrow makes you think of sorrow, and the sight of a full moon has afflicted the homesick hearts of travelers for thousands of years. On a silent evening when the brilliant moonlight floats bright and distinct over everything, the traveler realizes that she is not dreaming; she is simply a wayfarer, far from home. There are no anxieties, no regrets; there is no confusion, no hesitancy. Everything is clearly demarcated, real and compelling.

I wrote nothing about any of this for nearly half a year. It was only the next spring when I was writing a letter to a friend and quoting an ancient poet's words about moonlit nights that I wrote: Alas! Being able to appreciate great literature and taste life comes at a great price.

How great a price? I didn't say. And sensing the bitter anguish in that "alas" my friend didn't ask.

November 29, 1923

Dear Papa,

I didn't want to tell you that I was in the hospital. But I didn't want to hide anything from you, either. Besides, I'm feeling much better now. So I thought this might be a good time to tell you about what has happened during my illness.

Of course, it was the same old thing, , the illness Mama and I seem to share. I wasn't in any pain, so luckily, I really am just like Mama! Our hearts are the same, our thoughts are the same, and so are our bodies I love Mama so much I can even manage to love this illness.

But let me explain what happened. A few nights ago -- when it was very dull and dreary and I didn't even plan to get out of bed -- Miss S invited me to her rooms for dinner. Seated in her little study, we turned off the lights, lit flickering candles and sat there gazing at the blazing logs in the fireplace and telling Chinese stories to one another. Turning to one side, I suddenly noticed the pale yellow moon shining at us through the windowpane; it hung there in the sky, floating on white clouds that looked like gossamer strands of silk. Miss S also turned to look and gasped with surprise and admiration at its beauty. She hurriedly finished drinking her coffee and then we both put on our cloaks and went outdoors together. The moonbeams flowed around us like water, and the Milky Way was a scattering of stars.

Miss S pointed out the stars for me: The Spinning Girl was on that side, and that one was the Cowherd, and there were the Celestial Mansion, and Orion, and Castor and Pollux, and the Queen. Smiling, Miss S said softly: I've learned the names and positions of all these stars off by heart, and when I'm old and feeble and can't go outside, I'll lie in my bed watching the stars twinkling outside my window, and I'll feel just as happy as if I was getting reacquainted with old friends. Saying this, Miss S gave a gentle sigh. The moonlight shone upon her fluttering, silvery white clothes. Such loneliness and such poetic words! It sent a little shiver through me.

I asked her how she'd come to learn the names of the stars, and she said it was because her younger brother was a navigator. When she said that, I suddenly thought of my own Papa, of you.

I found myself recalling one night last winter, when I'd spent the evening sitting with Mama. Papa came home late, I told Miss S, and when I went out to greet him he stood there with me in the windy courtyard for a while, pointing out the different stars: "The Dog Star is on this side", he said. "And the Big Dipper is over there, and there's the Dustbin Star". I felt Papa's knowledge must be limitless, for him to know such tiny details about the vast heavens -- and that was a whole year ago!

Miss S accompanied my home in the moonlight, walking unhurriedly along the twisting path. We were both feeling melancholy -- and afterwards, I was ill for most of the night.

I did manage to get up the next morning, but I went back to bed after breakfast. However, that afternoon I went to my classes. When I came outside afterwards, the weather felt as if it was already early spring, so I decided to walk to the lake. The sight of the cold waves and bright ripples on the surface of the lake comforted me, and I made my way slowly to the water's edge. I was just about to sit down when I suddenly felt weak, and I fainted. By the time I regained consciousness, the sunset clouds hung like exquisite little wavelets in the sky. It was dusk by the time I got back. A few hours later, they found me lying in my bed and took me straight to the hospital.

The hospital building is on a little hill near the school, but arriving there in the middle of the night as I did, I couldn't see it very clearly. In the lamplight, the doctor and the nurse on duty peered attentively at me, and I tried to smile at them. Then I felt a strange sensation – but I spent a comortable night, and slept until dawn.

Very early the next morning, I saw the nurse carrying a huge bunch of blossoming yellow chrysanthemums that my dormitory classmates had sent. Seeing them made me remember how there were always flowers by my bed at home when I was ill and I abruptly burst into tears -- that was the first time I cried.

I slept during most of the day. But flowers and letters arrived continually, and before long, the whole room was filled with fragrance. There were roses, and chrysanthemums, and other flowers whose names I don't know. All of the letters were kind and caring, but I often didn't recognize the signatures, because I have so many classmates, and their names are so difficult to remember that I only know them by their faces!

I don't really mind being ill, here. The food is excellent, and the nurses are very attentive, and I don't need to worry about anything at all. There's even someone who combs my hair for me. My bed is moved several times each day. In the morning, they move it close to the window so that I can look out and see the red roof and steeple of the church, and the library, and even -- just barely -- the red autumn leaves on the trees on the far shore of Lake Waban, and even the outlines of the buildings beyond. There's a tall tree near the window, but I don't know what it's called. Yesterday morning, there was a colorful, red-headed woodpecker perched upon one of its branches. It stayed there for quite a while, then suddenly flew away. I also saw a little squirrel bounding back and forth beneath the tree.

Many of my classmates and teachers have come to visit me, but the doctor won't let any of them into my room. The nurses bring me notes from them, instead. So here I am, shut away in this little building -- my room is very fine, and more and more flowers keep arriving. I'm nearly surrounded by flowers! My mind is very clear, but blank. I haven't got any thoughts or feelings at all, except those of a compliant, obedient "subject" of this little "kingdom".

Sometimes, the telephone rings and I hear them talking about me.

" ... hospital ... her what? ... very serious ... not permitted to have visitors ... she's sleeping and eating very well, but the most important thing is rest ... wait until tomorrow before you bring any books ... flowers and a short note would be fine ..."

It's almost always that kind of talk. I listen vaguely, my head on my pillow. Now I remember how the telephone used to ring like this last summer when I was ill, and I can hear my little brother's voice telling people: "Sister ... oh, she's much better, thank you."

I feel I'm really a burden, causing everyone all this bother wherever I go. That first day, I slept and woke and slept again.

On the second day, I asked the nurse if I was allowed to write. She smiled and said that I could, but that I mustn't write too much. I was just glad to be permitted to write anything at all. The first letter that I wrote was to let the rest of the family know that I was safe and sound. I didn't want to keep anything from anyone, but I still didn't know exactly what had happened. The next letter was for my 96 American classmates in BB Dormitory. I wrote:

"Thank you so much for the letters and flowers that you've sent me. Lying here in bed, I feel almost as if I'm having a holiday as I look out at the sky, the lawns, the library and all of you coming and going through the church door, with the lake in the distance. Here in hospital, I haven't got ten pages of poetry to learn before class, and there's no morning bell to make me get out of bed. Aren't I lucky! Idly, I turn my back on the lines of poetry and gaze at the sun and the shadows and the stars, instead. If it weren't for missing all of you so much, I really wouldn't want to leave!"

The letters and flowers kept coming, filling up the whole room. When one of the nurses came in at dusk, she smiled and said my room had turned into a florist's shop, and I smiled happily back at her.

I've never really liked the fragrance of chrysanthemums, but I hadn't realized that when you combine them with roses they produce a lovely, sweet aroma -- and now I took advantage of the opportunity to enjoy it! The days seemed to last forever. Silence reigned supreme. The only things in the room were the flowers, and me. The rules and regulations said I couldn't have visitors, so I passed the time with idle thoughts and memories.

When I think of the things that have happened to me, each incident brings a happy smile to my face. I'm very thankful that for the past twenty years, the only thing I've ever had to feel sad about is being separated from you!

Miss B came rushing up from Boston to visit me. Thus far, she's the only person who has managed to penetrate this "forbidden zone". Although the doctor agreed to let her talk to me, he wouldn't let me say a single word. Miss B's face was pale and distressed, and her eyes were filled with tears as she told me: "I'd hoped we'd all have a happy Thanksgiving together. But don't worry. When you're better, we'll do something else ..."

I managed to remain calm and composed as I silently held her hand. She arranged the flowers that she'd brought and finally left, looking back at me again and again. As I watched her motherly figure walking away from me, tears trickled down my cheeks. That was the second time I cried

The best times were late at night. One night I'll always remember was filled with the fragrance of dense perfume. I asked the nurse to turn the lights on. There in the lamplight, all around my bed, pale green leaves and deep red flowers vied with one another for my approval, seeming to nod their heads and smile at me. In the silent sky beyond my window, stars twinkled and branches rustled in the breeze. Completely awake and aware, I felt as if I was one with the Universe.

I thought of two lines of poetry:

Enjoy the white lotus world
With the wind resting at its center.

But I was not able to enjoy this moment for very long! Sure enough, a nurse came in and opened the window. She pulled the curtains shut, and tidied the bed and then gathered up all of the flowers one by one. Turning back towards me, she smiled a very small smile, saying "They're too fragrant. The pollen isn't good for you and besides, your room should be cold at night."

I had no choice but to nod, and smile back. In the end, all that remained was a single rose left on the window-sill. There in the darkness, it seemed to know that it was the only one left to comfort me, and it continued to give out a warm fragrance all night long --

"If flowers fear the cold, why shouldn't I be afraid of it, too?" I only asked this question because I felt so disappointed. But of course I knew I didn't need to fear the cold, so I fell silent, and tried to be content.

I'd sleep so much during the day that I was wide awake at night. As it was too late for me to be allowed to read, I decided that I'd recite poetry instead. Listening to the sound of a passing train, I murmured:

> *Amidst the sound of trickling water in a neighbor's garden,*
> *The train is like a thunder-clap passing through a dream.*

Some friends gave me a book called The Student's Book of Inspiration. There's a line that reads:

"Nature's beauty is the most unforgettable thing in the world ... if anyone can add to it, Heaven itself will be proud of him."

It's true. Natural beauty is what we remember most of all. Today at dusk, Lake Waban's waters glittered like a sea of silver outside my window ... and what words can I find to describe how cold and clear they looked? In the autumn wind, the withered trees huddled together on the shore of the lake. But how can I possibly tell you how lonely and solitary they seem? And what words can describe the magical beauty of the autumn clouds? Or the fleeting changes of light and shadow on the square? Or my own, fluctuating feelings throughout this illness?

In the darkness -- which is still perfumed with the aroma of flowers -- I think of lines from another poem:

At death, do not remove the smell of orchids
At birth, protect the soul of jade!

Oh, dear! Perhaps I shouldn't have written that. I don't want to upset you. But I do want to you know exactly how I felt.

If I weren't so completely isolated and separated from everybody, I wonder if I'd enjoy reading letters as much as I do?

An American classmate wrote: I came back to school and went to your room, and it looked so empty that I almost burst into tears. Truly, if there's anything at all I can do for you, just say the word and I'll be delighted!

Another friend wrote: It's almost Thanksgiving, so get well soon! Everybody is thinking of you, and you're in all of our hearts!

I've had a letter from Japan: Life is uncertain. Although people can be very close in spirit, in the real world, they can be very far away from one another. Even though we are separated, I feel that you are very close to me!

And from a Chinese friend: How are you today? Do you feel like reading some Chinese books?

Only a few words -- yet they express so much. But my own thoughts were very muddled that night.. .

In the early hours of morning, the stillness was shattered by the horse-drawn cart that collects fallen oak leaves, and I found myself thinking:

The horse's hooves make a clip-clop sound
Its breath is like a rainbow.
The wings of sleep turn into a daytime goose
And I no longer care if the snakes in my dreams turn into
*   dragons!*
By now, the sky is bright.

Tomorrow is Thanksgiving Day. The branches on the trees outside my window are covered with ice. The water in the lake lies motionless beneath the first rays of dawn. It's winter weather -- People make their way along the paths across the common, one by one, all of them going home for the holiday. The American Thanksgiving holiday is like our Mid-Autunm Festival, a day when families get together.

Papa! I don't dare quote "Especially on festive occasions, we think of absent loved ones" -- not only because Thanksgiving Day doesn't really mean very much to me, but also because I'm ill, and feeling quite depressed today. I'm surrounded by the shadows that the flowers cast upon the walls, and by the perfume of flowers in the bedclothes, and by the misty, morning dew. Gazing silently out the window, I'm aware of a thousand things in my heart that I haven't the words to express, so I cannot help but weep --- and this is the third time.. . .

Luckily, I've never been one of those people who likes noise and bustle. When there's a holiday, I prefer to spend it someplace peaceful and quiet. So it's really a blessing that I happen to be here in this little building on this particular day. Impulsively, I pick up my pen and jot down a few words in my journal: Tomorrow is Thanksgiving Day. Everyone has gone off to have a good time, and here I am, shut up in this little building. And then I think of that line about the solitary flower in love with its own fragrance, and I can't help but giggle.. . .

The fragrance of the flowers seems to wind itself around my pen. It's been very quiet today, and I've been working on this letter, off and on, for hours. Lots of friends came to see me, but the doctor sent them away. Now, I can hear her talking on the telephone:

"Today she's reading Chinese poetry. She's resting comfortably, and quite content!"

I have to smile at that. Yesterday, I was reading poetry. But today, I've been using the poetry book to conceal this letter I'm writing. Papa, I'm afraid I'm being very naughty!

Suddenly, the nurse's crisp, white uniform appears in front of my bed. She's brought more flowers for me -- but she's also discovered what I'm doing. With a smile, she tells me that I mustn't write any more. I've no choice but to obey -- She's gone, now. She's really very kind. Watching her move back and forth about the room, words like "tall" and "graceful" float through my mind.

Papa, by the time you read this letter I'll be fit as a fiddle and out playing in the snow! So please don't worry about me! -- Give my love to the family, too! I'm always thinking of all of you.

I haven't finished writing, yet -- Papa, do you remember something that happened one night when I was little? I'd gone all the way up to where the flagpole stands on the hill, looking for you. Together, we made our way back down the hill beneath the stars, calling out to one another. How I loved you! That's how I feel today, calling out across the seas and oceans that separate us! Dearest Papa, we'll chat again. Perhaps I'll be able to write more tomorrow.

CONVALESCENT HOSPITAL

Seized by the sudden fancy that I heard a demon calling out to me, I sat up as if a whirlwind had spun me out of my deep, deep sleep …

A bell rang behind me, the door opened, and a silent, swift muddle of forms approached my bed. This surging blur gradually cleared– a doctor was standing there and staring at me attentively, without speaking. The nurse with him was carrying a basin, holding it with both hands. She gazed at me with shy, silent interest. I felt devastated, my soul a hollow void. The tears flowing down my cheeks seemed to be merely the result of some sort of pressure in my eyes, rather than caused by any emotion.

I seemed to see myself sitting there, partially propped against the rails of the bed; I felt as if a lump of ice had been somehow fastened to the front of my chest. Something was injected into my right arm, and in my secret anguish I could not turn away, although I didn't particularly want to turn away, either.

My blood seemed to have frozen in my veins, although my body suddenly felt very heavy. I seemed to sinking, layer upon layer, my body pressing down upon the railings of the bed, the bed frame pressing down upon the floor and walls of the building, and the building pressing down upon the earth.

Second by second, amidst all of this pressing weight, time passed. The people had drawn back away from my bed. The lamp at the side of the bed was turned down, so that all

I could see were the contours of the plaster walls – and at that point, I felt those plaster walls were all that remained of me!

I didn't even have the strength to shut my eyes – and then, inexplicably, I was dreaming.

In my dream, I was slowly making my way up through a multi-storied pavilion. I didn't seem to be treading on ground, but walking among clouds.

I don't know how far I walked, but I finally reached the highest storey of the pavilion. I raised my head and saw four words, written in gold: Feel eased and comforted. Now I understood that this was the southwest Temple of the Sleeping Buddha.

I moved forward involuntarily, and became aware of a great chasm beneath my feet. The darkness deepened. Music came from both sides, yet I could see no musicians. The music was like the sound of an alarm, like the urgent sound of pipes, random, cold and pressing, like a heavenly wind escorting me. In the dream I stopped and leaned forward and then sighed appreciatively. Truly, this was the magical, ancient music of the east!

I went further into the deep, dark interior of the temple. The darkness was like paint, like ink, and it increased with every step I took as I groped my way through it. The center of the hall was like a cave and I couldn't see the image of the Reclining Buddha. Suddenly a beam of light beamed down and revealed a white silk banner hanging high up on the wall at the rear of the temple. The banner was embellished with large, embroidered black characters which read: "The highest treasures of Heaven are open to man ..." The beam touched upon the character for "man" and then drew back. I was startled and backed away. Endless music surrounded me like mists or electricity as I plummeted down into a deep, bottomless pool …

As I fell, my soul rejoined my body. I could still hear the music ringing in my ears but I was back in my room, within the plastered walls. Outside the window, bright cold white stars were twinkling in the sky.

My body still felt as if it was made of ice but I also felt something - a little wisp of disappointment. If I can feel disappointment, I thought, I've returned.

It was still dark. As the effect of the drug that had been injected into my arm wore off I struggled to sit up, then leaned forward and picked up a pencil. Unsteadily, I wrote the words I'd seen in my dream upon a scrap of paper, and tucked it into the pocket of my robe.

I was so ill that I didn't know east from west. My soul had become a lump of ice.

I don't know if any other words followed the ones that had been so fleetingly caught in that beam of light, but every time I think of it I feel inexplicably sad. In fact, the meanings of many words only become clear in our dream. Those words were true.

December 5 1923
Shengbusheng
Convalescent Hospital
Wellesley

I often used to sit happily next to Mama, tugging at her sleeve and begging her to tell me stories about things that happened when I was a baby.

Mama would think for a moment, smile, and say softly:

"You'd already been ill several times by the time you were three months old. Whenever you heard the footsteps of the person who was bringing your medicine, you'd recognize them, and understand what was happening, and then you'd get frightened and start to cry. And no matter how many people might be standing around your bed, your anxious little eyes would fix on me and nobody else, as if you could already recognize your mother in a crowd!"

At this point, Mama's eyes would fill with tears. Mine, too!

"When you were one month old, you were carried out into the Ceremonial Hall and held up for everyone to see. You wore a bright, pink silk gown that your Aunty had given you, and a big, red satin cap trimmed with ribbons. I was standing with the other women of the family, and the sight of your plump, rosy face made me very proud.

"When you were only seven months old, we were all on a ship. I was standing by the railing, holding you in my arms. And suddenly, amidst the sound of the waves, I heard you say "Mama" and "Aunty".

Mama and Papa still don't agree about that story. Papa says that no child in the world can talk when it's only seven months old. Mama insists that the story is true. So -- as far as our family history is concerned -- it's still an open question.

"Once when you were sleeping, you heard a beggar wailing, and you thought she'd taken me away from you. You sat bolt upright beneath your quilt. You were covered in a cold sweat, and your face and lips were almost black. You were trying to cry, but you couldn't manage to make a sound. I came running in and kept trying to comfort you, explaining that it was only a beggar. But from then on, I didn't dare to leave you alone when you slept, unless it was absolutely necessary."

It's almost as if I can remember this incident. Whenever I hear about it, or write about it, I suddenly want to burst into tears!

"Another time, you were very ill. I spread a mat on the ground and sat down, holding you on my knees. It was during the summer. Papa was away. I spoke a few disjointed words, nothing that a three-year-old child would understand. Your amazing intelligence frightened me even more. I sent a telegram to Papa, saying I couldn't bear it any longer. And then suddenly a storm blew up and the three of us -- me with my worries, you with your illness and the exhausted nursemaid -- fell asleep. That storm seemed to snatch you from death's embrace and give you back to us."

I don't really think I was incredibly intelligent ... I keep reminding myself that a mother's loving eyes see signs of intelligence in every little thing her child does, especially when that child is her only, beloved daughter!

"Your hair was short. And you wouldn't stand still for a moment! In the morning, I could never manage to do your two little plaits properly. Papa always had to come and help. Stand still! Stand still! He'd say. I'm going to take your picture! And picking up the camera, Papa would pretend to take a photograph of you. This was the only way I could manage to do your fat little plaits."

And to think I'd never been able to understand why Papa wanted to take a picture of me every single day!

"Your favorite playmate was Aunty Chen's daughter, Little Precious. When she'd come to the house, I could leave the two of you alone in a room and take a nap. By the time I woke up, you and Little Precious would have put all of the toys away. I'd see two pairs of bright little eyes, staring at me."

Little Precious might have been my favorite playmate, but I don't remember anything at all about her. I don't even know her. But according to Mama, in those days I adored her.

"You were three years old, going on four. Papa wanted to take you to visit his ship, and everyone was hurrying to get you dressed and ready to go. When nobody was looking, you picked up one of your little wooden toy animals and tucked in inside your boot. Of course, you didn't know any better. But when you got to the ship, you insisted that Papa had to carry you. You refused to take a single step by yourself. Whenever Papa put you down, you limped. Everyone was quite mystified. Finally, when they took off your boot and discovered the little toy animal inside of it, Papa and all his friends burst out laughing -- silly child! Why didn't you tell anyone what was the matter?"

Mother would smile, and I'd also smile and then hide my face against her knee ... Looking back, it does seem a bit silly. Talking about something that happened ten years ago is a bit ridiculous, isn't it? But our silliness was mingled with feelings of warmth, and love.

"The thing that frightened you most was to see me paying attention to something else. To this day, I don't know why you were so terrified. But all you had to do was see me staring out the window, or even just sitting and thinking about something, and you'd shake me and cry out: Mama! Why aren't your eyes moving? So sometimes, when I wanted you to come to me, I'd deliberately sit still and pretend to be concentrating on something else."

I don't know why I behaved this way. Perhaps it was because Mama tended to concentrate on things when she felt sad, and I just wanted to cheer her up. But it's really hard to say. Whatever the reason for my behavior, it remains an enigma!

"On the other hand, you liked to concentrate on things, too. Every day at mealtime, you'd sit there and stare at the paintings and the calligraphy on the wall, or at the clock, or at the flowers on the table. It took you so long to finish eating that it seemed to the rest of us that you were counting the grains of rice in your bowl! It used to worry me. Finally, I moved everything that might distract you out of the room."

I do remember this. And it's quite clear that my liking for sitting by myself and thinking about things hasn't changed.

I'd smile when Mama talked about these things, but I'd often have tears in my eyes, as well. When she finished speaking, I'd rub my eyes on her sleeve and lie with my face pressed into her lap. At such moments, the world seemed to vanish; I felt that in the whole universe, there was only Mama and me; that I had actually merged with her, that we were a single being.

It came as a delightful surprise to me to gradually discover that this, in fact, was the truth. From the time I was created, Mama had known me, understood me and wanted me. Even before I knew that the world existed and I was a part of it, Mama already loved me. When I was three years old, I began to be aware of myself as an individual, to care about myself and think about myself; but Mama already knew everything there was to know about me.

Just imagine! If someone who was far superior to you knew you, understood you and loved you ... wouldn't it make you feel humble and grateful? Wouldn't you love her, and hope she will always love you?

One day when I was still very little, I suddenly ran up to Mama and stared at her and demanded: Mama! Why do you really love me? Mama put down her sewing, bent over and pressed her cheek to my forehead and said without a moment's hesitation: There doesn't have to be a reason. You are my daughter!

Who else in the whole world other than a mother who could say that? "There doesn't have to be a reason" -- and she said it so firmly, so unequivocally! She didn't love me because I was called Bing Xin, or because of any grand and worthwhile thing I'd done. There were no strings or conditions attached to her love. She loved me because I was her daughter, and for no other reason. That kind of love cancels out everything else, making other things seem insignificant. It surrounded me and enveloped me. Being loved so unconditionally made me into person I am today, and taught me to value myself simply because I am myself.

Knowing I am loved not only comforts and supports me, but spreads out to touch everyone who loves anyone and includes every mother and daughter in the world. I'll tell you something that is supposedly "profound" -- although most children know it. Love created the world.

No two things are identical. No two hairs on your head are exactly the same length. But whether or not you can see or measure it, a mother's love is a mother's love. Yours, mine, everyone's. A mother's love is immeasureable. Can anyone disagree?

I know it's not healthy to get all emotional after I've just been so ill. But I think you'll understand. Outside the window, autumn rain falls in fits and starts and the fragrance of the roses is silently singing the praises of their own mother, Mother Nature.

I can't sit next to Mama, now -- although she still loves me, there's nobody here to tell me stories about my childhood. So I've written to Mama saying, Please send me any little anecdotes about my childhood you can remember, and that I haven't already heard. Mama, I'm like an archeologist, using your words -- you, who know me so well! -- to study my own, mysterious self.

As for you lucky ones, you are still at home! So here's what I want you to do. When you finish reading this, put it down and run straight to your Mama. If she's gone out, sit quietly by the gate and wait for her to come home. But if she's in the house or out in the garden, go find her, climb into her lap and give her a kiss! And then say, Mama, if you've got time, please tell me about the things that I did when I was little. When she sits down, sit on her lap or lean against her knee and listen to wonderful stories about yourself, stories that you never heard before.

Then write and tell me all about it.

Maybe you feel sorry for me, because I'm ill and my Mama isn't here with me. But I'm glad I have a mother, and I'm glad I can remember all these things. Thanks to these happy memories, even the long hours of illness are bearable.

We'll chat again soon. Meanwhile, give my love to your Mama!

December 26, 1923
Sharon, Blue
Mountains

It's been several weeks since I wrote to you from the Shengbusheng Convalescent Hospital. And only a few days ago, I was so depressed that the only future I could see was hopeless and tragic. I never even dreamed that this magnificent setting of dark willows and bright flowers so much as existed. If only 'd known, I wouldn't have been so despondent.

I knew I'd been ill. But I've only just learned that this illness demands total rest. When the doctor rather off-handedly explained this, I wanted to scream. The mid-December new moon cast its desolate, lonely light across my bed, and the long, thin silhouettes of ice-laden white poplars stood in a tangled mass beyond the windowpane. I felt completely miserable, and utterly alone. All my plans for the coming year had suddenly become as ephemeral as soap-bubbles. I didn't even know whether I'd get well, or not. The autumn wind moaned, and my head drooped. The first time I found myself hating this Western moon was during the Autumn Festival. Now it was happening again. I never dreamed the sight of the moon could hurt so much.

The next few days passed in a muddled daze. When I woke up on 15 December, everything was covered with snow. The sky was full of flying, dancing snowflakes, the lake's surface gleamed white and my thoughts finally cleared. I stood silently at the window, gazing numbly at Lake Waban's pristine beauty. That afternoon, several teachers took me out in a horse-drawn carriage, although I was still in very low spirits. We galloped through the snow and deep forest, then up the Blue Mountains to this place, which is called the Sharon Convalescent Hospital.

There's no lake outside my window here. Instead, the building is locked in the midst of a thick pine forest, completely surrounded by mountains. It is absolutely still. Several times a day, trains come past and give off dense, white clouds of smoke that drift away between the mountains. Except for the sound of their wheels in the distance, there is total silence. And here I remain, thin and weak.

One by one, the days pass. I find myself thinking about the uniqueness of life. This is how it was before I was twelve years old, when I used to spend half the day at my books, and the other half at play. This is the first time since then that I've been forced to lay everything aside and come face to face with Nature. I read, I think, I admire the moon. The rosy clouds of dawn have become my daily lessons. Sometimes I wake up in the middle of the night, when the moon hangs motionless in the sky and everything is hushed and still. Looking about, I see only a blank emptiness. Contemplating, recuperating, being responsible only for taking care of myself ... now that I am facing months of idleness, my thoughts are free to range the length and breadth of the universe. No matter what happens in the great outside world, my only responsibility is to remain peaceful and quiet. How can I not feel grateful for such an opportunity?

During these endless days and nights, I find myself focusing upon even the smallest of things. In the morning, I compare the rosy clouds of dawn to determine whether or not they're all exactly the same. At night, I check to see if the stars have changed their positions. These things have become important to me. Just to the left of the moon, there's a very bright star that captures my attention every night. To the right of that star there are three more stars all in a row, twinkling down at me. I think they must be either the "Cowherd" or the "Spinning Maid". All the graceful, gentle stars of the autumn and winter are set out before me! Even when I close my eyes and sleep, they continue to shine down upon me, silently watching over my slumber until the first light of dawn. Only after they've entrusted me to the care of the rosy morning clouds do they sink silently, one by one, and hide themselves amidst the bright mists of day.

Speaking of the rosy, morning clouds forces me to lay my pen aside, for I cannot think of words fine enough to praise their beauty. All I can tell you is that the colors of the sky at sunrise change in exactly the opposite way as they change at sunset, when they go from light to dark, and from gold and red to deep blue and purple. At dawn, the colors change from dark to light; the blues and purples become a pink color that lifts the round ball of the sun up above the pine-covered mountains and into the sky, as all the creatures of earth awaken from their dreams.

Even in bad weather, when I lie on my bed and listen to the sound of the rain on the roof, I feel peaceful and tranquil. A couple of nights ago, I was listening to the rain when I remembered these lines:

" ... *at first, it was so hard to listen to the evening rain! Weary of travel, in a far corner of the world, my heart was filled with bitter, bitter thoughts ... The wine was gone and the way was endless ... Spent the night on the Chu River, the lamp flickering in the wind. Years of my life, lost in an alien land ... What a pity that time passes so quickly. The mournful wind and rain, these trees ... In the fine rain, I dream of returning, but it is so difficult to overcome these distances. Making cold music from a jade flute in this small building ...*"

These and other similar writing resonate sadly within my heart. But you needn't read these lines and you needn't understand them, or puzzle over them. When you grow up, you may very well write such things yourself -- but for now, there's no need to worry about them.

Although I don't remember much of these weeks in the mountains, the other twenty-two girls here all knew which day was Christmas! On Christmas Eve, they tied colored lanterns onto the branches of one of the pine trees standing in the snow in front of the hospital. They put a big star on top of the tree, and hung lots of smaller stars on its lower branches. At midnight, I was asleep in my bed as usual. Suddenly, I was gently roused from my deep slumber by the soft sound of Christmas carols. I opened my eyes. There was a moon in the sky, snow on the ground and between them, a big, bright star. It was as if the truth had suddenly been revealed to me -- the whole world seemed clear as a translucent, glittering crystal! I thought of that pure, innocent infant born on this night one thousand nine hundred and twenty-three years ago, of his absolute love of mankind, and his absolute sacrifice. This clear, pure, gentle moonlit night had been created for him.

My heart was ice, and my soul was water. Silent and respectful, I listened as the singing voices gradually faded away into the distance. Finally, all that remained were the vague sounds of children's happy carols coming from far away down the mountain. Slowly, I dropped off to sleep. In a dream, I saw my brother standing in front of me, holding a violin on his shoulder. Seeming both happy and worried, he enthusiastically played, How Can I Leave You? The music was thin as a thread, as if he didn't want to reproach me. Sighing unhappily, I woke up again. The sky was still heavy, but now it was Christmas Day!

The sun came out, and the snow on the tops of the pine trees reflected the pink colors of the sky, so that I seemed to be surrounded by red clouds -- just like an Immortal! I was thinking this when the nurse came in and pushed my bed along a corridor into a different room. With a smile she said, Merry Christmas! Then she brought in several dozen gifts, all wrapped with white paper and tied up in red ribbons, and piled them upon my bed. One after the next, I opened them. There were all sorts of games and books, and it took me nearly half an hour to open all of them. I was so happy that I felt like a little child, and wanted to go running to Mama's bedroom and wake her up and tell her to come and look. It came as real a shock to me when I realized that Mama was 10,000 li away ... suddenly listless, I reached out and picked up one of the books and leafed through its pages, but I didn't really feel like reading.

They don't usually light fires in this building, and it's as icy cold as the Arctic Ocean. Today, it was hard for them to get enough steam heat to warm the whole building, and perhaps they thought I'd be more comfortable in an inner room. I arranged my books and games neatly upon a table, but none of my brothers or friends were here to share them with me. The room was quiet. I looked at the snow-covered mountains in the weak sunshine outside the window, and thought of how things would have been if I hadn't become ill. I'd be in Washington or New York, surrounded by activity and noisy celebrations ... certainly not enjoying my solitude, as I was now. So once again, I managed to turn my disappointment into contentment!

That evening, the children who attend the school on the ground floor of this three-story building came along to a celebration in the courtyard. There were twenty of them -- they're all being treated here, and the school is run for their benefit. I still haven't been able to go downstairs, so I don't know many of them. In a few days, when they'll let me wander about, I'll certainly go and see how they work and play, and then I'll be able to tell you about how children here in the West enjoy themselves, even when they're ill. -- In the center of the hall, there was a brilliantly decorated Christmas tree with presents hanging from its branches. One by one, the doctor took them down. Each present had somebody's name written on it, along with a clever little poem to make us laugh. Even though the gifts were small things, the poems made them very interesting. I got a five-colored lead pencil with a little rubber cap on it, and a poem:

> You sit in bed, writing away
> And breaking the rules, every day,
> Leaving ink–stains where you may.
> So here's a pencil and a rubber, too
> Good tools for what you like to do,
> And a very Merry Christmas to you!

The doctor called the nurses' names as well as the patients' names, and soon the hall was full of people from eight different countries, all singing together in perfect harmony -- in a scene ablaze with lights -- singing loud and clear through a complete program of Christmas songs.

Tonight, everyone was a bit tired and went to bed early. Silence reigns. Far away, the stars still shine brightly down upon the snow-covered ground. I turn off the lights and stand by the window. Starlight pours into the room, bright as moonlight. I think about last night, how the children received their gifts in little groups of two or three and were totally absorbed in unwrapping the parcels. I'm standing there lost in thought when there's a knock at the door and a Greek girl comes in and exclaims, All alone in the dark, just like a poet! I didn't see your light, and I thought you weren't here!

I smile quietly, feeling as if I really had been out among the silent mountains.

This makes me start to feel homesick again -- but I won't write about that. By the time you get this letter, the Chinese New Year will have arrived. So I'll wish you happiness and peace!

December 31, 1923

Sharon, Blue Mountains

:

Bright light reflected from the snow fills the verandah, and reading Mama's letter brings tears to my eyes, as always. The branches of the pine trees growing on the mountains that surround us are thick with snow. It looks like fairy-floss. It gets so heavy that sometimes, handfuls of it slide silently off the branches and pile up on the snow-covered ground beneath them. Little pine trees! God has given you too much to bear! And here am I, my heart as heavy with love as your branches are heavy with snow, but unable to unburden myself.

You know, it's really strange that I've told you about so many things and yet haven't really introduced you to Mama -- so let me tell you what my brothers and I think she's like. She's the kind of mother whose every word makes us feel enthusiastic. Even when she writes, each dot and each stroke of her pen has the power to move us to tears.

I don't expect to feel unhappy when I receive a letter from Mama, but by the time I've read halfway through it -- and sometimes after I've read only one or two lines -- I feel so sad that I start to weep. Such depth, such sincerity, such enduring love! Such a desire to understand and appreciate everything in the whole world!

Here are a few phrases from Mama's letters. If she were your Mama, and you were thousands of miles away from her, how do you think you'd feel, reading these sentences?

"I couldn't help crying when I read your poem, To Mother. But then all your other letters arrived, and comforted me. (October 18th)

"Our souls are linked, so no matter what I am doing, I'm also thinking about you. (October 27th)

"We depend upon one another for survival, you and I. No matter where you are or what you're doing, I am there with you; surrounding you, protecting you, nurturing you and comforting you, all day, every day. (November 9th)

"Every night at dinner, my breath catches in my throat when I see the lamplight coming from your room. It's as if you're there, and simply haven't come to dinner yet. I'm just about to call you when I suddenly remember you're not at home any more. And then I feel terribly sad! (November 22nd)

"Your letter and photograph just arrived. I spent nearly the whole day reading and rereading the letter and looking at the photograph. And then when I went to sleep, I dreamed that I was with you. But how can any mother not miss her child?" (November 26th)

Each time I read such things, I feel upset. I even find myself wishing I'd never been born, so Mama wouldn't have to suffer the unhappiness of missing me. But when I think some more, I realize that even if I hadn't been born, Mama might have had another daughter, and would have worried about her. And I can't very well wish that Mama didn't exist! -- Besides, hasn't it always been like this, ever since the world began? As Mama says: How can any mother not miss her child?

Accepting this, I must wholeheartedly agree that ours is, after all, a very good world. A mothers' love is a force that can gaze upon a million upturned faces and recognize -- as if by magic -- the one person on earth who merits her help and love. And this love is like a raging fire, which tirelessly urges us forward, step by step, towards everything we achieve.

It's because Mama and I are separated that I'm thinking about it so much. Feeling surges like a tide inside of me. I sense the invisible link that connects Mama and me with every other mother and child on earth – despite being invisible, I'm absolutely sure it exists.

I didn't expect to feel like this before I actually left home. Nor did I anticipate that I'd spend so much time thinking about Mama. But I hope I'll always feel this way, and that even when I'm old, I'll be thankful for her love.

However, I'm not writing this letter because I want to talk about Mama but because I want to discuss the phrase, "a mother's love". Who hasn't got parents? Who is not human? Mother's love is always the same, and your experiences are as clear and true as mine. So don't think I'm being self-righteousness or proud just because my mother loves me ... after all, everyone has a mother. It's a bit like Heaven, I think, where nobody is rich or poor, and nobody is high or low, and God is like a mother, loving everyone. In the old days before time began, people weren't rich or poor, and there were no classes, and everyone lived free and content by God's decree, basking in the glow of what we now call motherly love!

Sometimes, I acted as if other things were much more important to me than Mama. I'd disobey her and argue with her about my brothers or my friends and even flowers or birds or books or clothes. Have you ever done that? Now I think that I must have been very spoiled and silly, for one's mother is the only person who will never be offended, no matter what. Lying here in bed, the mere thought of such incidents makes me terribly sad. So learn from my example, and be careful from now on. Your mother is the only person who loves you unconditionally, and every word she speaks is full of good sense. The love of other creatures and things comes and goes, but a mother's love lasts forever. Although there are many kinds of love, none of them is anything like a mother's love.

The snow has stopped falling in the Blue Mountains, and everything is clear and cold. There is nobody else here on the verandah, so it really is very quiet and secluded, with only an occasional peal of laughter floating up from downstairs. How deep and mysterious are the ways of God! He has lifted me up out of the shrill tumult of New Years celebrations and brought me here to toss and turn and think deep thoughts amidst the silent mountains.

As for my illness, I'm not suffering any serious symptoms just now. But I have not made what they call a full recovery, which will take time and rest. This letter is filled with things that I've wanted to write for months and that have finally escaped my pen ... perhaps that's a good thing, perhaps not.

On this last day of 1923, I wish you well.

> January 10-11, 1924
> Sharon Convalescent
> Hospital

Dearest Mama,

I don't know how you'll feel when you receive this letter. You have only one daughter, who lived with you for twenty years and sometimes she made you laugh, and other times she made you worry. Six months ago, that daughter of yours went overseas. Now she's ill, and writing this letter to you from the Sharon Convalescent Hospital.

These days, your daughter sits quietly in the lamplight, listening to the beautiful, sad, melodious music coming from downstairs, and to the laughing voices of the girls standing next to the balustrades. But your daughter does not go outside. She's been rereading letters she's received from friends in China, and suddenly, she feels overwhelmed. This is the first time since she came here that she's been so moved. In their letters, everyone asks how her studies are progressing and whether or not she went to Washington and Boston for the Christmas holidays. She doesn't know how to reply. The days seem to have flown past, and she has accomplished nothing.

Your daughter's heart feels as if it is tied in knots. She doesn't know where to turn for comfort. Her weak, tired wrist rests upon bits of paper as she writes, again and again, Farewells are unbearable. Then when the paper is full, she is astonished. Where has all that writing come from?

Mama! I shouldn't speak like this. My whole life has been filled with flowers and light and love. There have been only blessings in my life, never curses. -- But if you could feel the desolation of these days! And here I am -- I who have only known happiness -- trying to cope with these unhappy, silent, surging thoughts. Imagine a little boat, tossing amidst billowing waves, while the panic-stricken boatman clings to the mast and wails to the Empress of Heaven for mercy. Mama, my heart is like that little boat, trembling and quaking amidst the wild heaving of these surging thoughts. Even though you're 10,000 li away, merely writing the word "Mama" on a bit of paper makes my forlorn heart sink within me ....

Last night, I had written this much when Nurse came in and told me to go to sleep. Although I was feeling very melancholy just then, it's just as well she stopped me. Because if I'd kept writing in the mood I was in, who knows what sad things I might have written!

Mama, today there's a big storm raging outside. Earth and sky are white, and the grass and trees are bending their heads. At five this morning, the usual, beautiful, rosy colors of dawn had become wretched greens and wan reds. And it is fiercely cold! It was eight before there was any daylight, and the wind and rain have gone on all day long. One by one, everyone else has left the verandah and gone into their rooms, resolutely shutting the doors and windows. You can't even see the mountains through the dense, white mist. Suddenly, the rain bursts through the screen and beats against the windowpanes, splashing in through the cracks. The fierce wind blows the rain down the slope of the roof and flings it into the air like a fountain. This astonishing storm has blown my melancholy feelings away! A monotonous life needs shaking up -- It's just occurred to me that this is a bit like the way I felt on board ship, when I saw something extraordinary in the middle of the Pacific Ocean.

Our lives here are far too monotonous. Every day, we get up and lie down to rest according to the chiming of the clocks. Even our dreams are more interesting than our daytime lives. The green pines never change color, and the mountains that surround us on all four sides never alter. Suddenly, I find myself hating the pine trees because they're not like Chinese Ilex trees, which at least change the color of their leaves from red to white to green to yellow.

This life makes me think of my noisy brothers. Here, the girls just bend their heads over their sewing. Sometimes, it's so quiet that you can hear the sound of the needles going into the cloth! I amuse myself with sewing, but I don't use it as a substitute for lessons. I read a bit, write a bit, lean on the balustrade and watch the village children ice-skating or pushing their little sleds beyond the trees in the distance. One day it was so quiet that a strange thought popped into my head. I thought I it would be fun to buy a few big firecrackers and set them off, to give these silent mountains a bit of a shock and make them ring with sound -- Here, we don't even dream about firecrackers. I keep fantasizing about having something to play with that makes noise. In one fantasy, I have a little pistol in my hand. I load it, raise it, aim it and bang! Out comes a noise from behind the screened window! Even a little air-pistol would do the trick ... but of course, these are my secret fantasies. I'm not the only person here, and I wouldn't intentionally destroy everybody else's peace and quiet.

Mama! I'm in much better spirits now. Actually, the nicest thing about this place is the peace and quiet. People can't just come and visit whenever they please. They're restricted by the set visiting hours, and also by the snowy weather and the distance. Often, less than two hours a day are wasted in senseless socializing. I'm like a three-year-old child, busily playing and singing and saying idiotic things to myself here in front of the window, or in the sun-filled room or in the winding corridor. During rest time, when I can't sleep I sing quiet lullabies to myself -- it's exactly like being a child again, except that I haven't got my Mama here beside me!

My thoughts wander along this path or that as freely as those of a little child: Every day, as I lie on my bed and the nurse comes and pushes it out onto the veranda, I look up at her and imagine that the bed is my cradle and she is my nanny. I often gaze intently at the three brightest stars in the sky. Even when the other stars disappear behind the pale, wispy clouds, these three continue to shine. One of them is just a bit apart from the other two, and I imagine that it is the eldest of my three little brothers, just that little bit bigger and able to stand off by itself. The other two cling together, like my two littlest brothers. They're both still small, and although they rush about as they play, they make certain that they don't ever stray too far from one another, because they know they are young, and not very strong, and must take care of each other.

These three stars are always the first ones to appear after twilight, and the first ones that I see; they're also the last to fade away when the sun rises as -- after the other stars have gone -- they bid me a "temporary" goodbye! I feel a special bond with them, even during the day. At first, I thought I'd look in an astronomy book and find out what they're called, but I still haven't done so. Instead, I've given them names of my own. I call them Brother Stars, and each one is named for one of my brothers

Am I writing about my brothers, or about the stars? – Pondering this makes me think about the moon, beautiful and silent. In my imagination, it becomes Mama. When I wake in the middle of the night and open my eyes and see the moon high in the sky, it seems to be looking down at me, and nodding. I feel comforted, then; and I go peacefully back to sleep in its loving light. Of course, the brilliant and brave morning sun is Papa. Elegant and graceful, he rises from behind the treetops on the mountain opposite my window, saying with dignified warmth, Another day has come! And I sit up happily, and throw a shawl over my shoulders.

All the other constellations are also as dear to me as people, and I think of them with loving thoughts, just the way that I think of my friends. Perhaps I'm being childish, but I often think the only thoughts that contain true wisdom are those of children. I hope I'll always be able to think such thoughts, and feel such feelings.

Outside the window, the storm is still raging. It makes me think of a poem called, The Young Mystic, by Louis Untermeyer. I've translated it for you. Mama, if we were sitting here together and watching the wind and the rain, might I have said something like this?

The Young Mystic

We sat together close and warm,
My tired little boy and I --
Watching across the evening sky
The coming of the storm.
No rumblings rose, no thunders crashed
The West wind scarcely sang aloud;
But from a huge and solid cloud
The summer lightening flashed,
And then he whispered, Father, watch;
I think God's going to light his moon --
And when, my boy? -- Oh, very soon:
I saw Him strike a match!

The storm has still not abated. The rain beats down and the wind howls and the snow on the mountains has all melted. I want to write something else this afternoon, so I'll stop here. Mama, please pass this letter on to the newspaper, so that my friends can read it, too. Every time I think of them, I remember I owe them a letter. But all the bits and pieces I wrote during my journey are locked up in my room at the college dormitory, and the nurses have a dozen different ways to stop me from writing, and I don't dare disobey them. Yet all the same, I did promise I'd write to them, and it constantly preys on my mind. I'm not sorry that I made the promise; but I am sorry that I was so busy at first, and then afterwards, I got sick -- My homesick soul accompanies this letter, Mama. Truly, I can't write anymore. From a mountain far away across the sea, your convalescing daughter sends you kisses.

Sharon

Here in the moonlit forests of green mountains, it is an incomparable night! I can only compare it to the sight of a beautiful, serene woman, dazzlingly bright and colorful yet neither conceited nor flirtatious; a woman whose glance is modestly lowered, who wears a gown with gracefully hanging sleeves, and a jade necklace. A beautiful, reserved, serious woman.

In such liquid radiance, everything else is drained of color. The pine forest is a slab of dense blackness, while the sky is lustrous and transparent as white jade and the endless snow fields are a pale blue. These three colors become the lining of the cosmos, filled with condensed silence and natural dignity. Above them, the sky seems full of secret, sad spirituality ...oh, mere words can't describe it! It's almost as if the scenery itself refuses to allow anyone to stare at it, and will not permit its essence to be grasped or understood by a mere mortal.

An evening like this would not suit a general and his men, hunting at night —all those disorderly riders shouting to one another in the wind would trample and destroy the flat, fragile snow fields. And the singing around the fires and the raw, cold armor would outshine the cold, quiet moonlight.

Nor would an evening like this suit a lovers' quarrel — the whine of thin, pleading voices filled with sadness, uttering frail, weak words. No, human despondency and depression are much to "worldly" for a scene illuminated by glittering, translucent white moonlight and set among this vast expanse of trees and mountains.

Nor would an evening like this suit a troupe of elegant actors pacing up and down, one's beauty set off against another —among the trees and beneath the moon, you might see beautiful shapes and admire beautiful voices, but you'd be so enchanted by the cold and gleaming mists that your thoughts would go round in circles and not attend to the characters or the play.

Reclining upon a pillow, hemmed in on all sides by sudden sad thoughts, my mood abruptly changes and I feel quite depressed ...

Tonight's mountain scenery only suits sick girls like us, resting their heads upon their pillows and gazing up at the moon!

If I could fly to the moon and look down, I'd see long corridors winding through the mountains, snow pressing up against the railings of the verandah, and moonlight drenching the snow-white quilts and pressing down upon exquisite, delicate foreheads.

During these endless days in the bright mountains and towering pine shadows, the affairs of the outside world diminish and a new awareness dawns within us, filtered through minds that are clear as crystal. At such a time, wouldn't even the dullest-witted person find herself thinking deeply about things? So imagine how it is for all of these thoughtful, good-hearted girls?

It's like observing flowing water –in the moonlight, one thinks of home, and travel, and imperial Roman palaces alongside dilapidated houses and abandoned columns. One thinks of being at the Great Wall, standing upon the broken steps among the empty battlements; or standing beside the Jordan River, or visiting Mecca; or crossing Laiyin River or flying over Luoji Mountain. At this very moment, how many souls are freeing themselves and flying to heaven?

Thinking of the future is like looking up at a high mountain. You hesitate for a long time upon the road, you are so weary. Perhaps tomorrow, or later this year, the delicate web of sickness will break, and you'll find yourself rapping gently at death's iron gates.

Imagine paradise – is it floating upon Seven Precious Lotus Pool? Is it visiting the stars of the White Jade Belt? Are there joyous words? Is there fear, or cowardice? Are there earthly reunions, nostalgic recollections of human life, troublesome affairs in which one can succeed for fail, real hopes, vain hopes … what will we find in paradise? Not just you and me, but all living creatures – it is impossible to imagine it, after all.

All of life combined in a single instant, here and now, is only a sparkle of light in the flow of the cosmos.

January 15, 1924

While wandering idly along a corridor at dusk, I saw a sick girl. I stood in front of her bed and chatted with her for a while, and when I turned to look out the window I saw a single, twinkling star above the pine trees. The girl said, That's the first star you've seen tonight! Make a wish on it!

Then she softly recited this little rhyming poem:

> *Star light, star bright*
> *First star I see tonight.*
> *I wish I may,*
> *I wish I might*
> *Have the wish I wish tonight.*

Isn't that a lovely, gentle little poem? I can't translate it into Chinese for you, because poems like this simply MUST rhyme, and the Chinese words don't rhyme so it wouldn't sound the same if you recited it in Chinese. But I still want you to feel the way I felt when I first heard it -- so translate it for yourself, or ask someone older to explain it to you -- When she finished, I thought for a moment and then clasped my hands and gazed up at the sky and said: I wish my Mama, 10,000 li away, wouldn't worry about me so much!

Any day now, Mama will receive the letter about me being ill and in the hospital. I can just imagine what people will say, all the moaning and groaning! Yet now here I am, peaceful and completely idle, living the life of a floating cloud!

A few weeks ago writing to a Chinese friend, I complained that Sharon Sanitarium was as icy and cold as a cave made of snow, and that I spent each day battling the north wind. I asked, How can people sitting around their hot stoves possibly imagine what it's like here in this cold place on these cold days, struggling for life against Nature itself! Now I realize I was being a bit over-dramatic. After all, who ever heard of a life and death struggle as soft and gentle as this one!

Birth, old age, sickness and death are the most serious, most unavoidable events in anyone's life. No matter how great or noble or important you are, there's no way you can avoid these things. Now that I must face one of them -- sickness -- I can only wait and see what happens, and try to understand. Even so, when I imagine some invisible, gentle, unhurried hand penning my destiny, I can appreciate the imponderable mystery of Nature.

I used to hurry to Lake Waban several times a day and linger there, gazing at the sunset and thinking about my lessons. Sometimes I'd go rowing, and sit there watching the ripples in the lake, just wasting time. But as the wasted minutes trickled away like drops of water I'd start feeling guilty, knowing that I shouldn't have put aside my work just so I could come and enjoy the beauties of Nature. Perhaps God saw what I was doing and that's why He sent me this illness, so that I could cast everything aside and use the beauty and solitude of Nature as a cure.

And now? I live like a flower, spending my days growing towards the sun amidst soft breezes and gentle showers; I live like a bird, wandering and resting, moving up and down and left and right through my home in the empty air; I live like water, like a free, murmuring stream; I live like a cloud, rolling quietly along and drifting aimlessly upon the wind. I no longer have hundreds of pages of poems and essays to read, nor is there a little rowboat to distract me! I no longer stare lazily at the scenery, either. Even when I read the shortest of poems, I take my time and recite the lines again and again, and reflect upon them.

I love listening to the snow falling off the roof, and the pattering rain. And I love looking at the moon, and the stars. It used to be that I spent a lot of time worrying about ordinary, troublesome little things. But now I open my eyes and listen with all my might and concentrate as hard as I can -- I don't know how to describe it, but my awareness is like a moth leaving the cocoon, like an eagle circling in the air ...

Even if I don't deliberately listen or look, I can hear the melting snow and the rain upon the roof, and I can see the moon and the stars in the deep, blue sky. Now that I'm ill in bed, these things are my whole life. Yet before I became ill, I never seemed to have time for them.

The beauty of this story isn't that "One day you'll be able to go walking in the mountains" as one of the young doctors said to me. I didn't know how to reply to that. But it did make me decide to begin my stalled life anew from this minute on!

A narrow footpath winds its torturous way through the forest behind the mountains. Some sections are in sunlight, others in shade. I don't know how far it goes. I've only gone as far as the spot where there's a big rock where I can stop and rest. Climbing up on the rock and looking out into the distance, I can see mountain slopes covered with pine trees. Whenever I want to think about things, I take this path. I walk along by myself, my head bowed, listening to the dry leaves and the branches chattering away overhead. There's a thin layer of ice upon the grass, and it makes a rustling sound when I tread on it. At this time of year, the dim, gloomy hospital wards seem overshadowed with sorrow.

In front of the mountains there are endless hills, vast, empty and unoccupied, drenched with sunlight. At the base of the hills there's a lake, frozen solid and surrounded by more low hills and tall trees. This is where the children go ice-skating. (I'd love to skim along the lake with them! It must be like flying!) Whenever I want to think about the mysterious beauties of Nature, I take this path. I sit beneath the branches of the trees with the thin, warm sunshine upon my face, and I raise my eyes towards the glorious, silvery sky. I think about the vastness of the Universe, and the smallness of human beings. On my way back, slipping and sliding upon the ice and with the wind rushing past my ears, I feel as uplifted and happy as if I'd won a lottery.

One summer day three years ago when I was visiting the Western Mountains near Beijing, I wrote a little poem. I can't remember it all, but it went something like this:

> *At dawn in the deep valley*
> *You can speak to God.*
> *Beautiful as pictures*
> *Rocks nod their heads*
> *Grass and flowers smile greetings*
> *The divine force that created the Universe!*
> *In our starry, speeding future*
> *Along the way*
> *Hopefully, in the distance we'll find*
> *Other valleys, other dawns!*

Indeed, God did find other valleys and other dawns for me, but only after I left Beijing and traveled 10,000 li to Sharon. How can I have "not been in the mood" to understand God's purposes? I remember some lines from another poem about "footfalls in an empty valley" and the poem by Du Fu that begins:

> *Cut off from all -- only my beauty left*
> *My gloomy dwelling a hollow valley.*

I recite these lines to myself again and again, but all I can remember is

:

Sighing I wonder, amidst the grass and trees
What good is my parents' high-born name to me?

And I remember the last verse:

I pluck flowers, but don't put them in my hair
Amidst the cypress leaves my idle fingers bend
In the chill breeze, my silken dress so thin
As among bamboo thickets, the fading day doth end.

On my way home, I also recited:

Shapeless clouds swirl as if from a cave
As the birds fly wearily home
Into the mist
Comforting the solitary pine.

I think you should read the old poets very carefully. Sometimes, they speak the thoughts that lie unspoken in your own heart.

Spring is coming, smiling through the clouds. Soon, I'll have gentle, tender stories to tell. In my daily wanderings, I've discovered little broken places in the ice and flowing water. Just think of me roaming freely in all directions, uncovering Nature's hidden signs and tiptoeing into her immortal palaces ...

Despite this illness, I'm thankful; for my life is full of blessings. It's already rest-hour, and I'm lying here watching the stars. With joy in my heart, I wish you everything good.

P.S. There are green curtains hanging on all four sides of this large room. In a corner of the corridor, several girls are standing in front of the windows, joking with one another. The gramophone is playing lovely, light violin music. The girl sitting across the table from me is drawing my portrait, and she often asks me to look up. Sometimes, I am able to concentrate on my writing; but sometimes, I stop to listen to the music and the jokes. Now that I've read through what I've written, I think it's a bit confused. The beginning doesn't lead to the end. But the words came straight from my joyful heart, and I'm not going to change them, and I'll post this letter tonight.

February 4, 1924

If there's still some space in your generous heart, let me introduce you to a few special girls. I think you'll enjoy meeting them.

M is in the same ward as me. She's very innocent, and her nerves are very bad. Even the slightest surprise or alarm upsets and confuses her. She's been ill for over four years, and in all that time there hasn't been any improvement. Some days she'll feel a bit better, but by evening, she'll have a fever. As soon as she so much as sees the thermometer, I hear her muffled sobs. She has a wonderful home, but because of her illness she's been taken away from her family and must remain here -- My playfulness appeals to her. She often sits on her bed murmuring, "Papa loves me, Mama loves me, and I love ..." I have to really strain my ears to her what she's whispering, which is " ... and I love myself." Even when I don't feel like smiling, she smiles at me. She is so fragile, naive, and wretchedly unhappy that most of the other girls really pity her.

R is also in our ward. Everyone loves her, and she loves them. She's very good at embroidery and calligraphy, and can make lots of quite unusual and interesting things. For the past few days, she's been studying Chinese with me. On the first day, I taught her three words -- the Chinese words for heaven, earth and mankind. She said, You Chinese are such mysterious people! How can you possibly begin with such important words? When we start to learn English, we begin with words like dog, and cat. -- I just smiled, but I felt that what she'd said was remarkably significant. She learns quickly, speaks clearly and writes out the characters in a square, upright hand. She keeps track of the weather; she plays the organ at the Sunday church services; she reads newspapers to the other patients; and she's also in charge of the keys to the library. Her hair is cut so short that it barely covers her neck, she loves being outdoors, and she's been here for six months.

E is just 18 years old. Yesterday was her birthday. She hasn't got any parents, just an older brother. Over a year ago, her illness took a turn for the worse and she was brought here. She's a little better now, but she's still very thin and weak. She likes to call people Mama or Big Sister. She desperately wants to be loved, but she doesn't show it, and does her best to find small pleasures amidst her loneliness. Whenever the door of her room is open after the doctors have given her an injection, I see her all covered up and surrounded by pillows, tossing and turning and weeping -- what a birthday! What a life!

D is an Irish girl. Whenever I'd chat with her, she always wanted to know about my home and my family, and especially about Papa. At first, I wasn't really in the mood to be questioned like that. But later, her roommate told me that her father drinks, and often gets drunk and beats her. So her family life has been bitter, and very sad. In order to get away from her father, she had to go and live someplace else, with her grandmother. Whenever she hears one of the other girls talking to a member of their family, she always cries.

Yesterday, I got a letter from home. She just happened to be standing there and whispered enviously, Did your Papa send that letter? It's such a big, fat letter! Fortunately, I knew that she couldn't read Chinese, so I hastily replied, No. Mama wrote this letter. My Papa is quite busy, so he doesn't write to me very often. -- She blushed, and gave a little smile, and actually looked relieved. As a matter of fact, all of the letters I receive from home contain pages written by Mama, Papa and each of my brothers! I think that the worst thing that could happen to anyone is not to be loved by their parents. I can't imagine it -- even if I shut my eyes and try -- and I don't want to try. Poor, suffering girl!

A lives in the little building behind the hospital. At first, I didn't often see her. Then one time in the dining-room I happened to turn around and saw her looking at me, smiling slightly. From beneath long eyelashes, a modest, quiet, gentle gaze met mine, quite unlike the gaze of a Westerner! After we left the dining-room, I asked who she was and where she lived. And that evening, we spent half an hour in her room, talking. Her shyness and softness surprised me. When we were talking about seascapes, she actually presented me with a painting of a lighthouse. She's been here for two years, and they say there's been no improvement. All day long, she lies on the veranda facing the dense, dark forest beyond the little bridge, and the stream. She told me that when there's a storm and everything looks sad and lonely, she thinks this is all that there is to life, and feels depressed, and scared. I comforted her and she thanked me, but we both ended up in tears.

There are other patients ... but I can't bear to write about them.

This morning I woke up at dawn. The morning star gleamed faintly over the pines, and there was a thin mist. I sat with a coat draped over my shoulders and looked at the veranda and the little beds, one beside the next. On snow white pillows, dreaming girls tossed restlessly. I felt gloomy and anxious. All this seemed so futile! What good is all the love in the universe if these poor girls can't have some of it? They're ill and unhappy, and they deserve sympathy. I pray for them, but I'm just one small, weak individual. So I'm asking you -- even though you're 10,000 li away -- to add your prayers to mine!

I must tell you, some of my older friends don't approve of these letters. They say that I shouldn't write such sad, sorrowful thoughts. They say that it's not good for you to read these things, and that it's not good for me to write them, either. Of course I want you to be happy and peaceful; so this sincere advice makes me grateful but also ashamed. Yet life is more than just happiness and having fun. Things like falling ill and being parted from loved ones are the bitter juices that lie deep within the fruit of happiness. There is a dignity in serene sorrow. And there must be sorrow in life. Fan Zhongyan speaks of "innate sorrow and care" and Buddha said, "If I do not enter Hell, who will?" These things are the basic elements of everybody's life, to be heard, seen, felt and understood every day we live. So why should they be concealed from you, just because you're young? Although I've only experienced these things myself during the past six months, I don't think its wrong for me to write about them.

I'm stronger than the others here. I have a wonderful family, and I haven't always been ill. Not so long ago, I was able to travel halfway around the world, all by myself. I've not been bedridden like them, weak and weary with illness and spending all day staring at the green mountains. And anyway, I'm already far from home. At the university or here in the mountains, it's all the same to me. Of course, I'm glad when people come to see me; but when they don't come, I don't feel particularly sad or disappointed. But these girls are not travelers far from home, and it's only because of their illness that they're separated from their families. Wind, rain, snow and the difficult mountain roads often prevent their relatives from coming to see them. So they sigh with sorrow all year long and feel resentful with only more months of illness to look forward to. What sad lives.

And these are only a few of many others who are young, and ill. Perhaps you already know some of them. Isn't it everyone's job is it to help and comfort them? To see things like this and not be moved would be unbearable.

So, we do what we can: A bunch of flowers, a picture, kind words, solicitous visits, even something as small as a compassionate gaze. It doesn't seem like very much to you and me, but in the monotonous life of an invalid, when each day seems to last for a year, it's like a gift from Heaven. When the visit is over and the flowers are fading and we're already busy with something else, they -- confined to their sickbed -- are still grateful, and still remember.

I won't say any more. While I was ill, I received a number of gifts from you. Your loving hearts, and the books and gifts you sent all added "flowers to the brocade" and did me a lot of good. How can I possibly thank you!

Even though the unfortunate girls I've told you about are here on the other side of the world and far away from you, try to put yourselves in their place and imagine how they feel ... and be especially nice to any sick people you know at home. Think of the Immortals and "Use great thoughts to nourish your souls." Let these little stories temper your sympathetic hearts and make you capable of great undertakings.

Writing this letter on a windy, snow-swept verandah has left me with cold hands and frozen, sluggish thoughts. But reading through the letter I just received from my Chinese friends in Boston woke me up again! Is today the Chinese New Year? Are you all smiling and laughing and are there innumerable red lanterns and cups of wine? Here, there are only the silent, snow-covered, wind-blasted, empty mountains -- I won't write any more from this distant place, except to wish all of you a Happy New Year!

SHARON

Of course I love flowers!

Although we always had fragrant flowers at home, I rarely took part in activities like trimming their leaves and stalks and putting them in water. It was always Papa or Mama who had to fetch the flowers and arrange them in bowls. They'd click their tongues at me and say, When we see flowers in your room, we'll know Judgment Day has come!

If they'd been my grandparents I'd have paid more attention to such talk and stopped being so lazy – well, at least I'd have gone through the motions! But they'd speak and go right on with their watering and trimming. If they were setting out narcissus, even the bowls and pebbles would be moistened. I'd just stand there, smiling and watching.

It isn't that I dislike flowers, and I'm certainly not lazy. It's just that first of all, I knew my arrangements weren't as neat and tidy as the ones they made – I completely agree that arranging flowers is an art. And secondly, I liked things like this that led to running jokes between me and my parents.

But after I left home I never once forgot to water the flowers in my room. Look at the narcissus on my desk. Although it was planted at the same time as everyone else's, mine was in full bloom before any of the others had even begun to sprout. I cut many of the dense flowers and when the flower-tubes drooped I gently tied them up with a fine cord.

Then before they'd even finished blooming I'd become ill and was in the hospital, so I was separated from them, too! There was a little note from one of my friends which contained this sentence: I've watered your flowers for you.

Nobody ever mentioned them again, and I didn't dare ask. Lying there in bed I often thought of people going in and out of the building, and the flowers abandoned there in the silent room. I thought of Beebe Hall at night, beneath the moon. The only flaw in the picture was my darkened window, and in the dark room, nobody to admire the beautiful flowers blooming in the moonlight.

After I'd been in the convalescent hospital for a day or so I opened the little case that friends who'd tidied up for me brought, and was horrified to find the narcissus' green bowl inside. I realized then that during the three weeks I'd been ill the last petals must have fallen. Rather than "using my feelings to make poetry" I was upset – for quite a long time.

Three days later I received a little box. I cut the string tied around it with scissors and opened the lid. Inside there was something wrapped in paper and a card that said: Endless love, Anna.

Wrapped in the paper were scarlet roses. I treasured them. I put them in a vase and at twilight, their dense fragrance filled the room.

But the next morning I got up early, and noticed that the flowers were drooping. Their fallen petals were withered like cut-up pieces of black velvet! That's when I realized that the room was too cold for them. However, Ying's little building out back had a warm stove, and she needed comforting and deserved to enjoy the roses' perfume. So I immediately sent them to her as a gift – and I heard that within a few hours, their spirits had revived!

After this, gifts of flowers came one after the other. There were roses and narcissi, but I didn't have the heart to keep any of them. As soon as the visitors who'd brought them had left, I'd carry them across to the other building. I truly couldn't bear to keep the flowers I received and let them die in that place. Whenever more flowers arrived, I didn't even try to consider both sides of the question. I told myself that it was better for me to live simply. So I spent 60 days in silent loneliness, but I didn't sacrifice a single flower!

In February, another friend brought me six dianthus,

three red and three white, mixed with several stalks of ornamental grass. It was slightly warmer than usual that day. The friend who'd brought me the flowers stood there watching me arrange them, so I didn't dare take them away and give them to someone else. When they were nicely arranged, I put them on the table in my room.

When I saw Ying that evening I told her, I've got another vase of flowers for you! She smiled and thanked me.

I went back to my room to rest for a little while before going outside. When I looked at the flowers on the little table the white ones looked the same, but the color of the red ones had deepened and was poignantly moving. In the lamp light, the red, velvet-like petals looked like bright eyes shedding layer upon layer of refracted light. They were set off by the delicate green leaves of the grasses surrounding them, and the effect of the whole combination was utterly wonderful.

At the time, I didn't know if it was the flowers or the color that so tugged at my heart, but the feeling of love that welled up inside me was vast and deep …

I decided to stop being so silly. I'm surrounded by whiteness, I'm surrounded by cold, I never see the vital, red color of life and I've been living like this for 60 days! Why have I made myself so miserable?

I kept the flowers!

The next morning Ying asked What about the flowers? I just smiled at her, without saying anything.

There was a blizzard that day. I sat on the verandah, clutching my rug. I turned and looked at the flowers back in my room. The door and window were open, and the flowers rustled and swayed in the north wind. I watched, silent.

I went inside and took a book from the shelf, and

returned to the verandah. As I turned the pages, even the paper felt as if it was frozen. I raised my head and gazed at the flowers trembling silently in the cold.

By evening they were withered and ruined, their petals brown! It was too late to pity them, or mourn them. They'd already been sacrificed, by me.

I don't know if it was to comfort the flowers or to comfort myself, but I picked up my pen and began to write:

> *How much hope can be driven away?*
> *Cold snow, frozen winds –*
> > *Unbearably grieving for the fragile*
> *flowers*
> > *That joined me in my ordeal.*
> *How I pity them!*
> > *They made me forget myself.*
> *Truly, what bitterness is this?*
> > *Dianthus!*
> *My unthinking friend sent*
> *Magnificent, beautiful you*
> > *To accompany, to be relied upon in the*
> *cold*
> > *By isolated me!*

> *Broken blooms frozen in the glass*
> > *What I ruthless thing I've done!*
> *After two months in the mountains*
> > *The cold will leave my bones*

But cannot again …

That's as far as my thoughts took me. I put down the pen, raised my head and stared – spellbound – at the remains of the flowers.

I wrote about them several times, but never managed to really evoke them. The flowers were already dead, and there was no reason to gloss over the past. Later I found that draft of my first poem about them, tucked into a book.

March 1, 1924

Dear Bing

I've received your two long, sincere letters and they made me feel so much better.. Really, they did! "From a crack in the pine forest comes a sunbeam, and it's your brother's messenger come to wish you good health; listen to the peaceful evening breeze and you'll hear his voice." Dearest brother! I love you and thank you for your wonderfully comforting, poetic words.

Unexpectedly, I also received the book of poetry you sent me. It was more welcome than I can possibly say. Papa said he thought I already had it, and in fact I do have a book of selected poetry that's very similiar, but it's on the bookshelf of my dormitory room. I made a pitiful request for some of my Chinese books, but was given a hundred different obstacles and excuses why I couldn't have any of them.   It's as if they think that Chinese books are all full of difficult, abstruse philosophy and just to look at them will totally exhaust me!

I can't bear to defy the doctors and nurses -- after all, they mean well -- and in the end I just resorted to reading the few short poems that I'd brought with me to the hospital, over and over again. But then last night I received the book you sent, and I read it, treasuring each page.   What a sympathetic and understanding brother I have!

As for the poems themselves, they seem slightly delicate and fragile. And there were a lot of misprints. But overall, it's quite a good book.

You asked me whether I felt more moved by the poetic beauty of my surroundings before or after I left China. Afterwards, naturally!   In Beijing, one doesn't see the morning dawn against a backdrop of mountains, for a start. And also, travel seems to induce a certain state of mind that makes it easy to write poetry.

Once we'd sailed away from the banks of the Guangpu River and were in the midst of the Pacific Ocean, I wandered to and fro, all by myself. The blue sky and the jade green sea reminded me of these lines:

> *10,000 li of sea beneath me*
> *How can I not taste the bitterness of*
> *farewell?*

Leaning on the railing, looking past my fellow passengers and down at the waves splashing against the bow of the ship, a whole series of such sad thoughts filled my mind.

When I reached Wellesley, the frozen lake was my only friend. I walked there every day. On the day before Mama's birthday, I ventured out on the ice and looked at the water and felt very homesick. Suddenly, I remembered Zuo Fu's poem, Waves Washing the Sand.

> Soul supple as water, soft voices
> Green grass, fragrant land
> Peach trees green as jade conceal the red pavillion.
> It is spring. The soul of the mountain
> Calls to me.
> Dreams of home allow me no rest
> Provoking me, filling me with idle fears
> From one place to the next.
> An object cast into the water will float upon the sea
> Anxious to return home.

Feeling that the moment was very apt, I idly picked up one of the stones that lay along the edge of the lake. Using my little knife, I carved these two lines upon it:

> Dreams of home allow me no rest
> Provoking me, filling me with idle fears

Then I flung it as hard as I could, into the middle of the lake. Without looking at where it fell, I immediately turned and went back the way I'd come. But that little stone has been there in the lake ever since, and will stay there forever and ever, until the end of time. So long as the lake doesn't dry up, and so long as the stone doesn't rot away, the thoughts of home that I entrusted to it can never, ever be erased!

American towns are usually located at the foot of a mountain, or alongside a river. The houses are small and delicate. Outside the windows are fences, flowers and shrubs. It's just like the poem that goes, Beyond the greenery and the gateway, people live. But there are no walls around these towns, and the emptiness and vastness and open spaces are indescribably profound. Travelers on the road can look through the windows of the houses and see emerald green sleeves and gay dresses. And they can hear music, and laughter, and even snatches of conversation like: See how the sun is shining into the courtyard as it sets! It's much darker in the courtyard, now. Don't raise the blinds, it's too dark. The swings are inside, the path is outside. The Milky Way looks like a red wall, far away -- silly things like that!

Deep, dense forests lie between the stretches of open country. And the road winds up and down through the mountains like a snake. It's quite intriguing. I can imagine how it must look in spring, with wild flowers growing everywhere and making it even more beautiful. But even if you travel beyond the mountains, you won't see walled cities or Buddhist shrines. So all of my fine, poetic phrases like "Winding paths lead to beautiful places, to pavillions set deep in the grass and trees" and "In the flower temple, the faint, distant shapes of the Immortals, the hidden moon, the thin sound of the city bell" and "Atop a great mountain, an isolated city" and "Intoxicated by Jiangmen wine, we fall asleep upon the city wall" and "In the heavy mists of sunset, the lonely city stands, its gates shut" and "As if a curtain had been raised and stars scattered into the courtyard, the household stood silent, the bell-tower solemn and invisible" -- these make no sense, here!

In America, every place I see makes me think of a "brave, new land". But there are still traces of the original vast wildernesses and mountains, as well. At home, the cities all have a green, ancient solemnity about them. Perhaps it's merely the effect of old paint peeling off city walls and palaces, yet the sight of those ancient walls and palaces makes one want to simultaneously raise ones head in praise and bow down in worship -- admirable, beloved China, 5000 years old!

I remember last summer down south, at dawn in Suzhou, gazing out from the train at the city walls. When we entered the city. There was a damp mist over the river. A row of little boats seemed to stand guard over the town and multistoried pagodas peeped over the city walls. It was such a lovely scene! And I thought, I'm going to leave China and I'll never see this again!

As for life here amidst the mountains there's really no daily routine at all, except for reading and taking walks and chatting with the other girls. Here are a few lines of poetry that completely describe my life:

> *The sleep of illness allows*
> *One to vanish among clouds,*
> *And gaze down at cliffs and ravines*
> *Embracing human love.*
> *Once you've traveled to the Capitol*
> *You never forget the grave mounds and gullies*
> *Nor can you return to the mountains and rivers*
> *Without feeling twice as lonely as before.*
> *Lying in bed, comfortable, at leisure*
> *Filling the hours with brush and ink*
> *Resting my eyes upon beloved, ancient things*
> *Sleeping, eating, joking.*
> *Innumerable, wonderful, praiseworthy things*
> *To enjoy long life and good fortune.*

And these poems remind me of some lines from Du Fu:

> *Longing for home, walking all night beneath the moon*
> *Remembering my brother, sleeping beneath the white clouds during the day.*

And this, from Su Dongpo:

The idleness of illness is wicked,
But the medicine is even worse.

These too, perfectly describe my life at the moment ... there's no need to change a single word! All the green mountains are covered with pine trees, and the ground is covered with snow, and in the moonlight, everything is indescribably quiet and lovely. After supper, we often stand out front for a while. In the cold light, I can't help but feel homesick. And every day, there's a rest period from three to five in the afternoon. How can anyone manage to sleep in broad daylight? I just lie there, watching the clouds float across the sky. I often spend these hours re-reading my letters from home, trying to join my thoughts to those of my brothers -- Bing Zhang worries that I haven't been able to write enough while I've been ill. But even though I had to rest so much during my illness, my mind was quite clear and I've actually been writing more than I usually do. Now that I'm recovering, I don't have to take medicine. The doctors say that rest is the most powerful medicine. I've been reading a lot of old, Chinese poetry, but I haven't been writing much poetry of my own. On the one hand, I love ancient Chinese poetry. But I also sigh because I live a thousand years too late to "say the things that ancient poets have already said so well!" -- I've said too much! Whose fault is it that I've wasted all this time writing about the book of poems you sent me? Smile, that's supposed to be a joke!

Blue Mountain is very beautiful right now. On February 7th, just five days after the big storm, all of the thousands of pine trees were coated with a layer of ice. When the sun rose above the eastern peaks in the morning, it shone down upon the branches of these beautiful ice trees, giving off an unusual cold, bright light. Beyond the building, on the little path that winds through the snowy forest, someone is walking amidst the icy beauty. If he happened to look back, he'd see the curtains in my window. Despite the fact that high places are cold, this magnificent "jade palace" -- even though it's part of the real world -- truly challenges Heaven!

On the morning of the ninth day after the storm, they took me out on a sleigh. A pair of birds flew up into the sky and circled Blue Mountain, dipping and soaring. The track ran through deep forest, where icy branches stroked our clothes and brittle twigs snapped beneath the sleigh's runners. The snow covered everything. You couldn't see a bit of earth. Everything was frozen solid, without the tiniest particle of dirt or dust! Most beautiful of all were the white pearls of ice strung together upon the branches of the wild cherry trees. The contrast of the red buds and the white ice, sparkling and translucent in the sun, made me feel happy just to be alive.

Along the way, the women who were accompanying me pointed out the distant mountain ranges, rising and falling across the horizon. I suddenly realized how truly far I was from home, for these mountains are certainly nothing like our central plain -- Brother! I've always used the word "truly" as a figure of speech. But now that I think about it, many of the essays I wrote in China weren't completely "true" and the things I'm writing now aren't completely "true" either.

This is because I really do believe that in the end, we simply can't use words to describe the way we feel when we look upon the beauties of the natural world. No matter how great our longing for just the right phrase, no matter how many strokes of the pen, no matter whether we're speaking or writing, the expression we seek does not exist, and instead, we end up with the same old sentimental words and phrases. So we put aside our pen, and remain silent. But when these feelings refuse to go away, we feel that we must haphazaradly set down at least a few words so that we'll remember how we felt. And it doesn't matter that what we've written is little better than the records the ancients used to keep by tying knots in a rope or painting careless black lines on a sheet of paper. For all we've got to do is to look at these marks, indistinct as they may be, and past events will reappear before our eyes. And to be able to do that is satisfaction enough, I think.

Before I left China, I wrote a lot about feelings. But since leaving China, I have felt many emotions about writing. Although my surroundings are often very beautiful and deserve to be described, more often than not, I write nothing at all. In "Spreading a Net" Xin You An wrote:

For years I knew nothing of anxiety,
Yet I strove
And strove
To describe anxiety.

Now, I know anxiety.
And long to speak
And rest
But the world has turned to ice.

Truly, I now see my own soul without any illusions. Although the word You An uses is "anxiety" it's exactly what I mean! Without having known hardship, how could I write of emotion? Is it only me, or is it the same for everyone?

My Beijing Almanac says: On 15 August, clouds cover the moon; on 15 January, snow smothers the lamp. Last autumn, the moon was seldom visible, here. Yet on the 14th night of the first lunar month, there was a magnificent moon. I wouldn't have thought that an Eastern almanac could predict Western phenomena, so I expected rain and sleet! Yet every night after the 18th of the month, I awoke from my dreams to see the moon. Lying upon my pillow and looking up into the bright sky, my dreams seemed to mingle with the moonlight. The past few nights have been best of all. I wake up when it's nearly dawn. The sky is a dark, blue color and there's a golden moon ... and not far away, just past the moon's crescent, a single, gigantic star. In all the vast and cloudless sky, there is only the moon and that single star. It is an exotic, magnificent scene.

How was the Lantern Festival? I've heard all about the feasting at our family banquet! Mama was afraid I would feel sad, but I've used the jokes and cheerful words that you've sent to prop up my good spirits! So I'm feeling quite content.

I've come to the end of this sheet of paper, and there's really no more to say. But don't send this letter to be printed in the newspaper. It's just for you.

GREEN MOUNTAINS

There had been a blizzard that day. At dusk, I escorted a friend down the mountain, and then returned. We'd left parallel footprints, clear and distinct upon the fine snow. But as I came back along the road by myself, I looked down and saw only the neat, white falling flakes of snow; just like that, the footprints we'd made as we'd departed were already covered by the gentle snowflakes – looking out over this vast, white expanse, who would ever guess that a moment ago two friends said farewell, leaving their footprints just beneath this layer of snow?

Realizing this, I was overcome with sorrow! Su Dongpo wrote:
Where does a man's life lead?
He should be like the snow goose, treading mud and snow
Leaving a claw in the mud
To say that from here, he flew east or west!

But the poem doesn't tell the whole story; not only will the snow goose not return, but even the claw left upon the mud will not remain there forever ... because life is always uncertain.

In life, what is certain? And what is uncertain? Life is like a north wind that blows against us, flinging itself into our faces until we feel a great coldness that pierces to the very marrow of our bones; then it blows again, rustling swiftly through the forest and across the sky, indistinct and inconsequential, riding a flying horse from north to south, until it cannot be found anywhere at all.

Usually life leaves no trace, except upon a thin sheet of paper or (unlike time) upon an expanse of quickly-erased snow -- now I've made myself unhappy. Surrounded by the soft soughing of the wind in the pines I take up my pen again, and write of past events. The history of a life turns page by page, and gradually you reach the middle of the book, where every page is excellent and the colors are fresh and bright and pleasing to both the eye and the soul. This is God's own handwriting. I need only imagine it, and it opens before my eyes. Reverently, I add a couple of embellishments with my own pen.

Looking at what I've written, I sigh. Is man's life captured in the writing of a few past events? Moment by moment, that very life itself wears away whatever the pen has written ...

Here in the mountains, the spring rains are like wine for the pines.

May 9, 1924
Sharon Convalescent
Hospital, Blue Mountains

I haven't written in ages, have I? I know it's been a long time since my last letter, and this wasn't the way I intended things to be, at all. It's partly because the mail service between here and China is so slow, and so unreliable that letters often get lost. And while I was ill I feared that even if I wrote letters, they might never reach you. Besides, the doctors also insisted that I rest quite a lot, and I had to obey them.

It's just occurred to me that I've been away for nearly a year ... an anniversary! How quickly the time has passed. Despite the fact that writing such things puts me in a melancholic mood, I enjoy writing to you so much that I really don't mind. Besides, I'll soon be leaving this place. But before I settle back down to my studies, I want to go to some quiet place near the mountains and the sea, and live the life of a vagabond -- that'll make up for the six months I've spent shut up in stuffy buildings! I've taken advantage of the peaceful moments, and I've tried to be accurate, but I've had to rely upon my memory and there may be some mistakes in what I've written. So I hope you'll remember that I've only just begun to recover my strength of mind and spirit, and have just enough energy to touch upon the main points.

I've written ten little essays about my "Mountain Memories" for my younger brothers, and asled hem to pass them along to you. So, farewell! By the time I write to you again, I'll most likely have moved from this place.

INCIDENTS IN THE MOUNTAINS

The doctors call it convalescence, and I call it rest. Either way, I've spent six months shut inside this building, obeying their rules and regulations. Lots of touching, sad and even funny things have happened during these months, but they wouldn't interest adults, who'd probably frown, or roll their eyes, or just change the subject. But some of you will look at these stories and find them amusing and smile as you read saying, This is so good! And perhaps you'll tell other people about them; just the thought of that makes me tremendously happy! To tell you the truth, I've been quite bored for the past few days. Lots of things here just don't make sense. For instance, when the sun rose this morning I got up early and went for a walk, and it was so warm the heat made my head swim. Yet now although it's barely noon the sky is black with clouds and a fierce wind is blowing. I'm sitting here on the verandah, all by myself. So I might just as well spend the time writing.

*****

When I was little I was very timid, like most children. Grownups loved to tease me. My uncle told stories from "Strange Tales Of A Chinese Studio" about corpses and pale-faced ghosts and I'd listen uneasily, fearfully looking over my shoulder. At such times, I'd squeeze in among the adults so that I was surrounded, coughing apologetically. And at bedtime, I'd imagine I could almost see a ghostly hand stretching past my curtained door. Just the thought of it made me pull the quilt up over my head, completely covering me. And then of course I'd break out in a cold sweat that would last all night long!

By the time I was thirteen or fourteen, I was quite fearless. I'd wander all alone in the mountains, even after dark, barely noticing when the wind blew or the grass rustled. I wasn't even afraid to stand in the gloomy Main Hall of the Buddhist Temple, with the fearsome Guardians staring down at me. Mama often said that I was bold, whereas when she'd been my age she'd been gentle and timid.

I'm very resolute and calm in broad daylight. Invisible demons don't frighten me. But recently, in my dreams or in that moment between sleeping and waking, I've been suddenly gripped by terror and fearsome images seem to gather around me. I can't cry out. My hands and feet feel as if they've turned to wood. My very soul seems to shrivel. I struggle to wake up, and suddenly, I'm looking out the window at green, pine-covered mountains and a bright moon hanging in the sky. Shamefacedly, I smile – after all, I stopped having these kinds of timid, weak-willed dreams ten years ago. But I feel a bit sad, as well. For childhood is full of interesting things, and timid, weak-willed dreams are not the least of them!

*****

There is no schedule you have to follow, here in the mountains. So long as you turn up on time for meals and to have your temperature taken, you can do as you please.

The doctors and nurses don't care how you spend your time. It really is like being a child again. You can do whatever you want.

America is not my native land, and Sharon is not my home. It is just by chance I became ill, and have had to spend six idle months here. When I do leave, I'll probably never return. And I think, one day I might be sorry if I don't preserve some of these memories. So almost every day, I bury things, and dig them up.

I loved to do this when I was little. When something amused me -- a little boat sculpted out of cuttlefish bone, or tiny figures cut out of colored bits of paper -- I'd bury it. Or I'd write characters on a leaf, and hide it in the earth. Or I'd carve characters on a rock, and then throw it into the water.

If I thought of it again, I'd go back and dig it up and look at it. But if I didn't. it just stayed buried forever.

When you're ill, nobody expects you to act like an adult. So what harm was there in acting like a child again? I'd walk around in the mountains by myself, and at various times I'd leave different things in different places; a visiting card, a scenic photo of West Lake Wind, an old gauze kerchief, things like that. I spread these items across the mountains like pieces on a chessboard. I put them beneath flowering peonies, alongside bubbling springs, in mountain pavilions. It made me smile to think that they were there, hidden in those places. If I felt like it, I'd sometimes dig them up just to look at them.

Occasionally, I encountered other people. When that happened I'd stretch out my muddy hands and stand up, furtively. It would have been very difficult to explain what I was doing. When they asked, it was no good to speak and no good to remain silent, so -- having no other alternative --

I'd just smile. This made the other girls more curious than ever, but I kept my secret.

When a friend came to visit me, I jokingly told her that I was becoming more of a child than ever. I blushed, but I didn't mind. I liked it that I blushed. It's true that this reappearance of my childhood self sometimes made me wonder, but after six months of rest and feeling full of natural spirits and energy ... what's wrong with a little blush?

* * * * *

We had a lot of blizzards last winter. When it stormed, we'd sit in the Main Hall and joke, or chat, or play the phonograph or the piano or just braid one another's hair, anything to pass the time.

Sonya was Greek, and a little younger than me. We were often together. She considered herself to be a member of the ancient races – like the Chinese -- and sometimes we joined forces and joke with the American girls, pretending to laugh at them.

I couldn't play the piano, and she couldn't sing. But being quite bored and not having anything better to do, one day we wandered over to the piano and managed to pick out a simple little tune. Everyone else teased us, saying, Stop before you make fools of yourselves! What kind of music is that?

Sonya crossed her arms proudly and stood there in front of the piano. What do you know about music? She asked them. This happens to be a combination of the ancient music of the two oldest civilizations in the world! It's an instrumental ensemble, and you ought to appreciate it!

I continued to play the piano. Sonya kept singing

loudly and as other girls were trying to talk, everybody finally got really annoyed. They covered Sonya's mouth and pushed her into a corner and blockaded her in with chairs. Soon, the room echoed with laugher.

Afterwards, even if we played tunes like "Indiana Moon" or any of the other American songs we knew, at the first sound of the piano the other girls would nod and smile and say, Listen to the ancient music!

* * * * *

We continued to sleep on the closed verandah, even when the thermometer fell to 18 below freezing. Every night, the stars were our closest friends. They were only spots of glittering light but we were accustomed to being able to see them and when we couldn't see them, we felt dull and restless.

During blizzards, we couldn't see the stars. One snowy night, Helen and I sit facing one another at opposite ends of the verandah, clutching our quilts.

Helen pointed at the sky and said, Look! There's Venus! But when I looked, I saw that it was just a light from the winding, mountain road. I grinned and pointed at another twinkle of light in the mountains and said, And there's Jupiter, over there!

The more we looked and pointed, the more lights we saw. The windblown lamps here and there in the deep pine forests all became constellations in the sky. And in fact, the snow was falling so heavily that it was difficult to tell where the mountains and trees stopped, and the sky began. Those innumerable flickering lights might easily be stars. They looked the same.

But the lights we saw were here on earth. Our illusory stars didn't move as the hours passed. All night long, they stayed in the same position.

Even so, during those nights when the blizzards made us feel lonely, our make-believe stars comforted us!

* * * * *

There are many things you're not allowed to do during Rest Hours. For two hours every afternoon, you have to lie there on your bed in broad daylight, even though you're not tired and don't feel like sleeping,. It is so disheartening.

I'd often sneak a book into bed with me, to read. I'd wait until Nurse was making her rounds, and then I'd quickly slide the book flat beneath my pillow, shut my eyes and pretend I was asleep -- no matter how rebellious I felt, I didn't dare to openly flaunt the rules. And all I ever did was read. But there was a girl named Bea who frequently got up and sat on her bed with her hands clasped around her knees, amusing us all with her chatter and jokes.

Today, she sat up again. She saw there was nobody on duty, and did an imitation of the doctor. Everyone else was lying down watching her, and giggling. Nurse came down the corridor, but Bea's bed was at an angle and she didn't see Nurse until it was too late. All she could do was stand there, embarrassed.

Nurse entered the verandah. We were silent, not daring to say a word. Nurse asked Bea, Why aren't you lying down? Bea said, My stomach hurts. I think it's gas. When I lie down, I feel sick. Nurse asked, How was your appetite today? Bea had the nerve to give a worried little smile and say, Not very good! Nurse sighed deeply, and left the room. Bea turned to look at us and holding her head in her hands said with a rueful grin, Now I've done it! Just wait and see!

Sure enough, Nurse returned carrying a cup of medicine. We could all hear it fizzing. Bea had to swallow it. The rest of us buried our faces in our blankets and laughed until we could hardly breathe.

Nurse stood there watching until Bea had swallowed all of the medicine. Then, she slowly left the room. Dejected and holding her stomach with both hands, Bea lay down on her bed.   Half-laughing and half-crying, she exclaimed, Gosh! That was vile!

She didn't say anything else. But having to take that awful medicine when you weren't even sick was really too much!   Everyone laughed and applauded, saying, You've been punished!

* * * * *

The children in Sharon called me Eskimo, and I think it's the nicest and most interesting nickname that I've ever been given.

The Eskimo are a fierce race of native people who live in the North American forests. They have black hair, wear furs, make houses out of snow, and live by hunting and fishing in cold, snowy places. How could I ever be as brave as them?

Ignoring the winter winds and snow, I often played in the forest and walked past the frozen lake below the forest where the village children went ice skating. We saw each other again and again, but we never spoke. However, they'd always stop playing and turn to gaze at me, and whisper to one another.

One day the doctor's niece told me that the village children were saying they'd seen an Eskimo come out of the forest. When they were asked why they thought they'd seen an Eskimo, they said it was because they'd seen someone who had black hair and was wearing furs. The doctor told them the person they'd seen wasn't an Eskimo at all, but a convalescent patient from the hospital. So they weren't frightened anymore.

If I was a real Eskimo, my thoughts would be much simpler than they are. That's enviable, I think. I once read in a book that modern people do more thinking in five minutes than primitive people do in a whole year. Physiologically, we haven't improved in 500,000 years. But our ability to make things and to think about things just grows and grows. That's our misfortune, and the source of all that's wrong with mankind!

I'd be happy to live my whole life in the forest, my bare feet treading upon dry twigs, sitting quietly and listening to the whisper of the leaves. Cool breezes from beyond the forest would be laden with the fragrance of pine branches. I'd be quite alone, surrounded by vast, white fields covered with snow, There would be nothing to see or hear but the green pines and the white snow. I'd love that!

Just before I left the hospital, one of the other girls said jokingly, When you leave here and suddenly find yourself surrounded by Boston traffic, don't be scared. Remember, a year of being shut up in a place like this can make you practically unfit to live in the real world!

As you can imagine, I already felt apprehensive. Now that I'm healthy again, day-to-day things are filling my life ... but deep inside, I'm still an Eskimo. Black hair and fur are merely external details.

* * * * *

The old doctor with grey hair said, I'm pleased you're already so well. But the city won't be good for you, this summer. And neither will the sea.

His words were shattering.

You don't have to learn everything you know from books. And I didn't care if I never visited crowded places like New York, Canada or Chicago. But when he said I couldn't go to the beach, I was heartbroken.

I looked up at him and said I couldn't see any reason why I shouldn't visit the beach.

He smiled and replied that he didn't want me to go to the beach because it was too damp, and not good for someone like me who had only just recovered her health.

We argued about it for half an hour. Finally he said, All right! You can go for one week! He added that spending autumn on the lake would be good for me, too.

I do love Lake Weibing, but only because it reminds me of the sea. So seeing the lake instead of seeing the sea won't make me feel any better.

Unfortunately, after six months at Sharon, I hadn't even seen the lake. All I'd seen was a tiny spring. And although mountains are nice enough, they're simply not comparable to the sea. I have my reasons!

People often use the expression, "vast as the sky and boundless as the sea". But you can only feel the full extent of this vastness and boundlessness when you're actually on the sea. Traveling through the cliffs and rocks of mountains, you sometimes see little more than the occasional shaft of sunlight. Even when you reach the top of a mountain, the sky is a separate thing and the boundary between the mountains and the sky is jagged and uneven, nothing like the flat line of the horizon where the sea meets the sky.

The sea is blue, and grey. Mountains are yellow and green. Mountain colors are not superior to the colors of the sea. Blue and grey carry subtle connotations of solemnity and distance, whereas yellow and green are simple, limited colours. True, we often think of yellow as an honorable color because the Emperor's imperial robes are yellow. But we call the Emperor the Son of Heaven, which means that we honor Heaven even more than we honor the Emperor ... and the heavens are blue.

The sea moves, but mountains remain still. The sea is active, while mountains are rigid and inflexible. During hot days, when old people sit and stare at the green mountains, the black, motionless slabs of rock look like sick cows. But no matter when you look at it, the sea is never still! Slight, crystalline waves roll continually from the horizon to the shore, joyfully splashing against the rocks and cliffs, rising and opening into thousands of bright, silveyr flowers!

The sea is all around us, but so are the mountains. Comparing them with one another is like comparing flavors. If you read ancient poetry, you'll see what I mean. For example, ancient poets who watched the moon rise over the mountains and over the sea wrote:

South Mountain fills the world,
the moon is born of stone".

Think about those lines. They describe a rugged mountain, but isn't this description also like a description of someone who is too fat to move, or numb with cold? Those lines don't fill you with delight, do they? But:

> The moon rises over the sea
> sharing the horizon with the sky.

Which is also about the rising of the moon, gives us an image of remote, resplendent brightness!

Admittedly, there are no red, white, purple or yellow wildflowers growing on the surface of the sea. There are no lovely blue sparrows, or little, red-breasted robins. But during autumn and winter, the wildflowers fade and seeing them wither and fall makes us sad. On the other hand, dawns and sunsets upon the sea allow the water to reflect endless reds, whites, purples and yellows. And these are flowers that bloom throughout the four seasons, without stopping. And as for birds ... yes, red-breasted robins and blue sparrows are lovely. But the sea has gulls, white-breasted with green feathers, gracefully floating on the crests of the waves, "mincing with tiny steps across the towering waves, their silk stockings gathering dust" Looking at sea birds, I also tend to think of the ancient eulogies praising beautiful women like: Proud as a roving dragon, ephemeral as a shy swan!

Being at sea also gives you a certain perspective about nature. Leaning against the railings and looking down, you can't help but think of what might be beneath the boundless, glazed expanse of blue; bright pearls, corals, mermaids, sharks? In the mountains, very few people think about the gold, silver, copper and iron that may lie beneath the rocks and yellow springs. But because sea water is transparent, people's thoughts naturally tend towards the depths.

The more I write, the more examples come to mind. But to make a long story short, I think the sea is vastly superior to the mountains. And if that short sentence mortally offends the divine order of things, let me atone by killing myself – but by leaping into the sea, not by throwing myself off a mountain!

Discussions are so interesting. If you want to disagree with what I've said about the mountains and the sea, that's fine. After all, "men's minds are not the same, and each believes according to his own" There are many differences and variations in our world. If everyone had the same face, we'd never need to look at anybody! And if everyone had the same likes and dislikes, and wore the same clothes in the same colors, it would be as if the world had turned into a big school, with everyone wearing the same uniform! The thought is not only funny, but unappealing. By the same token, if everyone loved the sea then everyone would go sailing, and I'd never have it all to myself!

* * * * *

The mountains are like walls, and the grassy areas between them are like courtyards. This belt of mountains and forests is my playground.

Just after dawn while the clouds are still as lustrous as pearls, I go roaming about outdoors until my shoes and stockings are drenched with dew. And late in the afternoon when I get up from my nap, I pace the mountain roads at dusk like a wandering cloud, letting the soft breeze waft through my short skirt and rolled-up sleeves.

It's like the poem:

At sunset, on a fragrant, grassy slope
I loosen my saddle.
Nobody to admire the flowers with me
Nobody to drink wine with me
Nobody to care if I get drunk!

But that's really not a good way to be. It's sometimes quite difficult to live through times when "nobody cares". And even if you do manage to get yourself into the right sort of mood for wandering through mountains, you'll find it difficult to maintain that mood in other circumstances. It's not easy to pretend you're a drifting cloud upon a river when you're at school or in the middle of the city -- there are too many people telling you what to do!

This morning I went and visited the Childrens Ward behind our building. Inside, the children were at their lessons. Some were writing out vocabulary words, others were doing sums. Everyone was busy at a task, yet in the midst of all that busyness they still managed to pass hidden notes to one another or to whisper secrets or jokes. Their little hands and feet were never still for a single moment. I knew all of them, but because they were at their lessons I just sat quietly at the back of the room and didn't dare to speak to them.

Sitting there made me realize that I hadn't seen a blackboard for six months. Then, the sight of the big, round globe on the teacher's desk and the child-sized desks and chairs and the books with large print and rounded corners took me back fifteen years. On the blackboard were these sums:

35	21	18	64
-15	+10	- 9	x69

Standing in front of the blackboard I tried to do these problems, pondering, my head resting against my hand. A little boy with a piece of chalk in his hand gestured wildly, and I felt even more distracted. Sunbeams moved gently beyond the window, and even though I didn't have to stay and do lessons I found myself looking at the big clock on the wall and impatiently longing for the moment when its hands would tell me that class was over.

When the class finished, I chatted with the teacher. The children circled around us, approaching and then drawing away. One of them giggled and asked, Do the people who live in the big building have to do lessons, too? I said, No. All we do all day is play. Someone else exclaimed, You're really lucky!

They're convalescents, too; but even so, they have to attend class for four hours every day. As I'm only allowed to go for walks at certain times of the day, those are the only times I see them.

I think of myself 15 years ago, and I feel ashamed. Three times seven is twenty-one, four times seven is twenty-eight ... I've been through it all, learning how to recite the multiplication tables and being shut up here, as well! And then I think back to how things were just six months ago; big, fat notebooks, shelves and rooms filled with reference books, professors' words flowing like water ... now that I'm better, that life will begin again.

Life goes on. People used to tell me what to do, and now I tell myself what to do. "Yellow sorrow big as an implacable spirit" ... so long as other people are telling you what to do, there's still time for passing notes and whispering and joking. But when you're telling yourself what to do, there's no longer any point to that kind of thing. It has taken just ten years of training for me to become a person totally subjugated by books!

So, am I lucky? It's not so simple, is it?

* * * * *

Machines have their places and their uses, we all know that. They save effort, and they do heavy work very quickly.

Idle and unoccupied as I am here in the mountains, I've not managed to escape machines. Even mowers are machines, although they can be operated with just one hand. One day, I went out front to watch the farmers sitting on their machines going at full blast as they chugged their way slowly across the distant fields. All it takes is for one of those machines to pass over it, and even the hardest dirt looks as if it's been turned into waves and is divided into rows. In less than half an hour, a broad area had already been plowed.

The farmer took a watch out of his pocket and looked at it. Then he unhurriedly turned his tractor back towards the field. That's when I left. I don't know why, but I found myself feeling amused. Although the farmer was using a huge tractor, his tiny watch was the machine that was really in command! I thought it was very funny.

When I was a little girl, all you could see beyond the walls of our family compound were wheat fields. The cultivation and harvesting of the wheat were quite common sights. Squatting on their heels in the fields and covered with perspiration, the farmers and their wives were either driving their hoes into the ground or harvesting the wheat with sickles, one stroke at a time. Watching from the side, I often sympathized with their strenuous efforts and felt it was a shame that it was such slow work.

Looking at it from both sides, I tend to believe machines are tools that contribute to the happiness of mankind. But the other day, I found myself wondering about this.

Yesterday afternoon, many of the sick girls in this building didn't get any sleep at all. During our Rest Period, the air was filled with the ya-ya-ya noise of tractors going back and forth in front of the building. In the suffocating summer heat, lying on our beds felt like being in a steam furnace; and all the while, the dull, monotonous, deafening, continuous sound of these iron machines was pounding through our skulls. Between our own feelings of restlessness and anxiety and the noise and vibration of the machinery, we felt as if we were being about to go mad!

Resentful murmurs were heard throughout the building, but there was no way to stop the machines. I ended up with a terrible headache. Downstairs, a few of the girls were feverish and I felt particularly sorry for them, thinking all this disturbance must be making them even worse. A dozen sick girls were forced to spend half the day suffering, just to save the farmers a half day (or maybe even a whole day) of work ... Comparatively speaking, there is no comparison! So you see, machines don't necessarily increase the happiness of mankind.

When I was a child, only a wall separated my study from the wheat fields. If the farmers had been using machines back then, I wouldn't have been able to study at all!

The racket went on until dusk, and then it finally stopped. My head hurt, so I thought it might help to go for a walk. I found myself actually walking past the very machine that had not let me rest for hours – and when I reached the edge of the field, I saw a few farmers standing there uncertainly, rubbing their backs and shaking their heads and sighing. In fact, the tractor had broken down. But because it was so heavy and cumbersome, even ten men weren't enough to move it. Tomorrow, they'd have to get another machine to come and tow it away.

When I went back inside, I was smiling.

* * * * * *

The girls all laugh at Pauline and say she's a simpleton. But she isn't, and I really like some of the things she says. For instance, once she said, Talking to people is so limiting. I'd rather talk to birds, or kittens. They don't hassle you, and what's more, they listen gently and quietly when you speak to them.

I often see Pauline sitting under the cherry tree, looking at the little birds and talking and laughing to herself. Sometimes, she sits on the verandah stroking a kitten and doesn't move for hours at a time. I honestly don't see anything wrong with this, but perhaps this behavior is why the other girls call her a simpleton. I don't know.

There's really no reason to be uncomfortable when you talk to people. But sitting properly and politely and talking with strangers or adults or professors isn't much fun, either. And every day over the past ten years, I seem to have spent more and more time being proper and polite. Even though I grew accustomed to it, I still wished I could set myself free. So during these past six months, I've often been a bit of a simpleton myself!

My first joy was pulling up grass and feeding the horses. When you watch these enormous beasts meekly grinding their big, soft mouths as their large teeth eat grass from your hand, you can't help but find them appealing.

Every day I used go to the cow shed behind the mountains where the big, gray horses were housed with their milk carts, to feed them. And when the milk wagon stopped out back and the driver was carrying the milk into the kitchen, I'd approach his horse. Bowing my head, I'd kneel down under the cherry tree and pull up some brocade-like leaves. The horse would turn his long, narrow, friendly face around and look at me with welcome anticipation. We gradually became acquainted. When he saw me from a distance, he'd raise his head. I think that after I went away he thought of me every day, even though he couldn't say so.

There was also a little dog. It was brown, and whenever it saw me, it barked threateningly. One day, I was walking in the snowy mountains and to my surprise, I encountered this little dog at the top of the hill. He chased after me, barking furiously. Scared, I stopped and stood very still. He could see I was terrified. He stopped barking and with the air of having won a victory, lowered his tail and loped away down the mountain. I watched him go with a sigh of relief, and went back the way I'd come. But my heart was pounding and I didn't sleep well for three nights.

The other girls told me he was really a nice dog, and never used to bark at anyone. So when I encountered him the next time, I called him by name and he came to me, wagging his tail. From then on, he accompanied me whenever I went walking in the mountains, running ahead of me or behind me. With deep snow covering the forests and everything so cold and still, he made me feel quite brave.

There was also a cute little black dog who liked to jump and play, and a tame, gentle little white dog.

I've never been particularly fond of cats, because they're cunning, sly creatures who like to scratch people. There was a little cat at the hospital. When I woke up the morning after I'd been admitted, it had jumped onto the bed, quietly curled up on my chest and gone to sleep. It must have got in through a hole in the door. Now, I really hate the sound that cats make when they're sleeping! I thought about pushing it off, but I was afraid it might scratch me. During the past few days I'd been very upset and anxious, and this was making things worse. Luckily, it wasn't long before the nurse came in. With a distressed look on my face, I asked her to please pick up the cat and take it away.

However, I gradually became fond of it. The little cat never scratched anyone. I'd watch it lying on its back in the grass and using its two little front paws to play with rose petals, and then frightening itself and getting all excited. It was such a lively, happy little thing.

But the most delicate and exquisite creatures of all were the little birds. In Beijing, all I ever saw were crows and house sparrows, although once in a while I spotted a woodpecker. But here, whole flocks of birds arrive as soon as the snow starts to melt. First come the bluebirds. Westerners think bluebirds are a symbol of happiness. That makes sense to me, because the bluebird's sweet, melodious song announces that spring has arrived.

Red-breasted robins are even more common, perching on the snow or on the grass, bright and cheery. The honey sparrows are much smaller. Flying up from the trees, they're even smaller than the buds on the branches.

Sometimes when I look up and catch a glimpse of them, I stand absolutely still, holding my breath and not even daring to move my eyes lest I frighten these delicate, fragile little creatures.

And there are lots of other birds with bright, beautiful plumage, but because I don't know their Chinese names I can't tell you what kind they are. Even before the sun rises, the lovely sound of birdsong rises from the mountains and valleys. When the moon is dim and a breeze stirs just before dawn, I lie there in bed listening and feeling utterly content. Spring belongs to the birds. I think of two lines of poetry: "Birds sing the spring" and "In the spring one's eyes are never dim and there is birdsong everywhere" -- now, I really appreciate those lines!

Here -- where the high point of our day is having our temperature taken -- we truly love these little birds.

Bluebirds and the robins build their nests in clumps of roses, and in lilac bushes, so low that you can touch them with your hand. I often go and visit the birds' homes, but I never steal eggs or catch nestlings or do anything to disturb their happy households. I think about what a short time it's been since I left my own home, and how worried Mama and Papa would be if somebody caught me and shut me up in a cage so that I could never return – wouldn't they be heartbroken? I care about the fledglings as much as I care about myself, and I love their parents as much as I love mine.

It's interesting to see how the baby birds hatch out of their eggs. They have little yellow beaks and only a few feathers, and they're actually very ugly. They're very hungry, too. All day long they sit there in the nest with their beaks open, chirping and wearing out their poor mother who must continually fly to and fro. But eventually they grow up, and then their mother encourages them to fly to the ground. Their feathers are fluffy, their little wings flap and wobble and compared to their mother, they're quite plump. The muddle-headed little things don't know what to do, so they dazedly follow their mother. When she happens to peck at a little bug, they all come running, chirping and struggling to be the one who gets to eat it. At sunrise, the mother bird teaches them how to sing. Her voice is sweet and tuneful, but their voices quaver. Even so, within a few days they've learned to fly, learned to sing and learned to search for their own food so that they're no longer wearing their mother to a frazzle. When I visited them the day before yesterday, they weren't there. They'd already gone off and built nests of their own on nearby branches. They often visit their parents.

Even some of the insects are loveable. There are little, pale pinkish-grey butterflies, and tiny snails with little round shells on their backs. Bees buzz, green frogs croak in the water every night, and fireflies twinkle amidst clumps of flowers. They're all soft, gentle and innocent. If you're nice to them, they'll be nice to you. Adults are busy and have no time to play with them, so they love children.

July 14, 1924

Traveling in New England

:

It's already been ten days since I left the Blue Mountains, days I've spent at the lake and by the sea. Yet in a strange way that I can't quite explain, a part my soul is still in the Blue Mountains.

I ended up spending the first big summer holiday in the hospital. On the Fourth of July, I was still waiting to leave. Naturally, few festivities took place there in the mountains, except at dusk, when the little patients from the children's ward paraded down the mountain, carrying red, white and blue flowers, waving American flags and singing the national anthem. When they passed the front of our building, we all applauded.

That night, everyone said goodbye to me, laughing and giggling in spite of their own sad situations -- and when it was time to go to bed, I discovered my quilt was covered all over with little things that felt like rocks. When I looked more closely, I saw that they were actually dozens of baby pine-cones. Luckily they were still soft, and didn't hurt me, but I had to laugh. We're always playing little tricks on one another, and on my last night, everyone wanted to do something memorably mischievous.

The other girls ran away, laughing. I didn't chase after them, because I was already tired, but -- still giggling -- I carefully brushed all of the little pine cones off onto the floor. However, my quilt still smelled like a pine tree! So that's why they were all urging me to go to bed, I thought. So they could play this trick on me! I got into bed, but I couldn't sleep. I watched as wave upon wave of smoke and fire gushed forth from the tiny villages far below. The sky glowed red, as if heaven was lit by candles. Seeing and hearing the fireworks, I felt quite content.

It was slightly overcast when I woke up the next

morning. I got up very early, and walked quietly around the mountains. I looked fondly at everything, at each tree, at each flower, at each place that had been significant to me: the little shelter and the bridge over the flowing brook; the pine forests towering to the sky; places where I shed homesick tears; where I sat reading aloud in the silence of the early morning; where I picked Lady Slippers and gathered leaves; where I wrote my essays, and letters. For me, the entire atmosphere was one of rest, and purity.

When I finally departed at dusk, there were more tears. Although I wasn't really unhappy, I couldn't help feeling a bit wistful. The other "wild geese" stood in a row beside the door. One by one, they shook hands with me. Amidst the waving white handkerchiefs, I could hear them ringing bells to see me off. I saw traces of tears upon their faces. Why must life be so full of goodbyes?

As our bus reached the summit of the mountain, I looked back through the window at the white building set in a sea of greenery -- my snow cave, gradually disappearing into the sunset. But I'd been cured of my illness, and I was already beginning to forget my unhappiness and all those pessimistic forebodings of looming catastrophe.

I feel nostalgic about Sharon, as if it were a stretch of water, simple, and innocent. It shielded me and sustained me so I could get well. It was like a wet nurse. I don't love my wet nurse as deeply as I love my mother, or as tenderly as I love my friends, but I still feel deep emotion whenever I think of her.

Sharon also allowed me to experience four things that I'd never truly known before

The first of these is Weakness. Unable to sleep or eat as usual during my convalescence, I'd often get upset and then my temperature and pulse rates went up. I was never completely convinced by the saying that "healthy minds live in healthy bodies" or that it was too much studying that made me ill, no matter what other people thought. But now I understand how closely body and mind are related, and how greatly sickness and weakness can upset even the calmest sous. That's why I obeyed doctors' orders, and now I can feel spiritual strength returning like water gently rising. Are any of you placing too much emphasis on intellectual things? If so, I hope you'll listen to me, and not go down the same, disastrous path as I did.

The second thing is Cold. Cold is really quite intriguing! And what's even more fascinating is the fact that I didn't really feel cold. It was only when I saw my visitors curled up and shivering, and sensed their amazement at our lives here amidst the wind and snow that I realized how cold it really was. My experience of cold was mostly numbness. My eyeballs seemed frozen, and so did my clasped hands. But frozen eyeballs can still read, and numb fingers can still write. And you should have seen us laughing and playing in the wind and snow! We pulled sleds through the snow, marched against the wind with the pine forest staring down at us, wore snow masks upon our faces, and sometimes waded through snowdrifts up to our knees! Surrounded by whiteness, I wanted to shout: Wonderful! After three months of dashing around in freezing cold winds and snow, I think about you inside your warm houses and in front of your hot stoves and can boast, I'm not cold in three feet of snow. Now, I'm tougher than you!

At night, the moon is as cold, bright and unyielding as bone. Its face is like ice. The moonlight makes the earth seem frozen, and immobile. The cold moon and the glacial clouds are dazzling. Although I'm snug and warm beneath my sturdy quilt, everything else in the universe is freezing cold. Living in these conditions is like being a fish in water. Waking from a night's sleep, I discover that my breath has formed a layer of ice upon the outside of the quilt. And when I sit up, bits of ice fall to the floor with a tiny, tinkling sound. You see what I mean when I say it is intriguing. And I now understand the saying about "hot tears turning into ice."

The third thing is Idleness. Although it is sometimes be fun to be completely idle, the difficult thing about it is never knowing what tomorrow will be like. At Sharon our lives were like characters upon a printed page, one following the next, carefree days passing one after another. Before I became ill, scheduling was a real nuisance, as nearly everything had to be planned at least two weeks in advance. You'd think all that planning would be enough to make anyone feel depressed! Westerners live their whole lives according to schedules, hurrying about busily all day long, even when they're having fun! I got caught up in this whirlpool, too. But during my months at Sharon, I could quietly erase the word "schedule" from my dictionary, and this delighted me!

Idleness also gave me time to write. When I wanted to take up my pen, I did; and when I wanted to put it down, I did that, too. I'd never experienced this feeling of being able to write as freely water flows to the sea and clouds drift across the sky. This is the thing I will remember most vividly about my time at Sharon!

The fourth thing is really two things combined. They are Love and Sympathy. I want to be quite serious about this. When you're suffering the bitterness and anxiety of illness, love and sympathy are the most comforting things in the world! I used to think that sympathy was something we were obliged to learn how to feel, while love was something that just came naturally. I also think that I took these feelings for granted. I suppose that so far as family -- our own flesh and blood -- are concerned, this is probably right. Our love for members of our family is unconditional; blood ties are unconditional. Among friends and fellow students, love doesn't necessarily appear, but depends upon luck and greatness of character. And true sympathy is rare. Yet during this long period of sickness and convalescence, my friends were very sympathetic and solicitous, and even braved the wind and snow to come here and visit me. And they weren't just going through the motions, or doing these things grudgingly. Some of the doctors brought me bunches of flowers, and chatted with me about being ill and so far from home, and even wept with me. These are the kinds of feelings that make us human beings; these are the kinds of feelings that created the world. How can I explain how much it meant to me? When I was ill, people gave me love and sympathy; and now I've learned how to give love and sympathy to others. If it's made me into a more "giving" person, mine was indeed a worthwhile illness!

"Fellow feelings among fellow sufferers" -- what a meaningful phrase that is! We all felt sorry for one another, and this created a supportive atmosphere of mutual love and protection. If one of us had a fever, or developed some new symptoms, everyone commiserated. We'd stand at her bedside, silently holding hands, murmuring sympathetic words and then just gazing sadly, our eyes filled with compassionate tears. We had come to this place from the four corners of the world -- what did we have in common? Only in illness did we find the empathy that truly allowed us to know others, and to know ourselves. Despite the fact that we were of different races, we were intimately linked, one to the other. How can anyone know love and sympathy unless they've experienced life?

Love and sympathy lie on either side of the road of life. They are fields that can be sown at any time; they can blossom forth at any time; and the journey of life is enhanced by their fragrant flowers. Thanks to them, travelers can push through branches and brush against leaves and step upon thistles and thorns, yet feel no pain. They may sometimes weep, but they never despair.

The longer we live, the more we must endure. I think we sometimes feel life as a sharp, piercing needle, whose every stitch draws mortal blood. Who has not felt life's mystery and magnificence? Who can escape life's endless joys and sorrows, partings and reunions? I have not yet gone very far along this road. So there's plenty of time for happiness, and I know it will come.

There are thousands of books where I am staying now, and dozens of musical instruments, and although I can choose among them, I haven't touched a single one. As it is such a long time since I've seen water, I spend as many hours as I can at the lake or the sea. Now that I'm near water again, those mischievous urges I felt while I was at Sharon seem to have vanished ... and I sit quietly, my head bowed over my embroidery. But on the other hand, if you ever want pretend that you're once again a child, you really do need to be surrounded by mountains where nobody else lives.

I've still got lots of things to tell you about my excursions to the Atlantic Ocean, but I've written so much already that I'll leave the rest for next time. Be happy!

July 22, 1924
New England

As our bus speeds along the shore, I watch glittering golden rays from the setting sun spill out across the surface of the water. There's an evening breeze, and my summer clothing seems too thin. But how lovely this life is, after having been so ill!

Wherever you go here, you are never far from water. You wind your way along roads that are so smooth they seemed to have been polished. At any moment, you might glimpse an expanse of sparkling water just beyond the dense shade of the trees. My favorite place is Spot Pond -- although to call it a pond is a bit inaccurate, as it is as large as a small lake! -- there are four small islands in the center, with little wild trees growing upon them. The pond is surrounded by a deep, dark green forest. That first night after dinner, I went for a walk to recover from the long bus ride. Suddenly, I thought I could see beautiful people amidst the fragrant grasses! It was just like the poem about, "Magnificent beings beside the water". In fact, it was a crowd of young people, hand in hand. The boys were wearing collars that looked like scrolls, and the girls wore bright, summery dresses, and had bobbed hair that waved in the breeze. Their light, gentle laughter echoed across the water and in the wind. It was so romantic, so natural and so free!

Mystic Lake, Spy Pond, Horn Pond and other places are also very charming. All the lakes are "radiant and enchanting". Gentle breezes upon the water create endless folds of rippling wavelets, and all kinds of fragrant grasses grow along the shores. There are green forests, smooth, even roads and winding pathways. It is pleasant walking at dusk, gazing into the distance and enjoying the coolness; and the setting sun reflected in the lake is magnificent. When you return at night, two rows of starry little lamps on the bridge sway gently to and fro, cool and twinkling. The full moon is as bright as daylight. Imagine the magical brilliance of the landscape!

A few days ago I visited Revere Beach on the Atlantic Ocean. Tourists covered the sand like ants; sitting down, standing up, playing in the water, all of them wearing swimming costumes. A fun-fair stretched for about a mile along the edge of the beach; loud music and a hubbub of voices. Children rode on iron cars and horses, and there were rides that spun around, and colorful little blimps. When the ride starts, the little blimps go soaring up into the air, one after the next! The children really love it.

But the beach gradually seemed to me to turn into a sea of people, swarming like insects, so that you couldn't see the waves or the salt spray. I didn't much like it, so we turned the car around and went on to Nahant.

Now, it again became quiet. While we were still in the forest I could already feel a sea breeze. Two or three more turns in the road, and the rocky seacoast lay before our eyes. This is how the sea really looks, its true face; an incredibly vast expanse of blue, towering, bottomless waves, and a strong, gusty sea wind that smells of raw fish. Sniffing the sharp, fishy scent of the sea I found myself remembering how we used to collect sea shells when we were small, and how we used to marvel at the sheer vastness of it. Facing into a wind that was almost strong enough to blow me away,

I felt that I understood the sea in all of its serenity, all of its irresistible, awe-inspiring wonder.

Between the jagged rocks and just below the trees that grow in the crevices of the cliffs, I could see Egg Rock and its white lighthouse. It was very quiet just then. Summer villas stood here and there among the broken cliffs. The sea breezes that penetrated the forests seemed to be playing a tune of "heavenly winds and billowing seas". I sat with my cheek resting on my palm, lost in thought, thinking of these waves going all over the world to the European countries, a host of dragons without a leader; and eventually making their way to my own peaceful land, even further away than the sky and the sea.

We have no magnificent lakes at home; no vast Atlantic Ocean, no dense, green forests, nor fragrant, grassy footpaths. All we have in Beijing are roads with clouds of dust flying up everywhere, and muddy little alleys, and ash-colored walls, and perspiring rickshaw boys running back and forth. My Beijing hasn't got anything much at all!

But don't worry. I won't forget to retur home. Although this is a happy, free time for me, I'm still just a tourist. In a letter to Mama I wrote -- Beijing seems to be a place that hasn't got anything at all -- but it has my love, even if it hasn't got anything else. And if it has my love, it has everything! All the people I love most live within its ash-coloured walls. And the billowing clouds of dust let me breathe in the scent of home ...

Yi Bosheng wrote "The thoughts and emotions of

sailors are as turbulent as the rise and fall of waves". These were the thoughts that came to me as I sat quietly upon the cliff, one after another, rising and subsiding like the waves of the sea. Then the evening star appeared, and the sea winds seemed to want to blow me back home. On the way back, I felt a bit listless. But I did buy a basket of freshly-gathered clams. When I asked the barefoot child alongside the car who was carrying the basket how much it cost, he just turned his rosy-cheeked little face towards me and grinned. I silently blessed him, wishing him happiness as boundless as the sea itself.

Speaking of water reminds me of Lake Waban, and the day I brought a Japanese friend back to South Natick. We passed through Wellesley, and as the car sped through the campus grounds I saw Shengbusheng Convalescent Hospital, its doors and windows closed, standing there on the mountain. Although I did manage a slight smile, the thought of all the weeks I spent there made me feel quite dispirited. When we went to have a look at the silvery glimmer of Lake Waban, I only glanced at it. The walls, the buildings and all the rest of it still seemed to swim before my eyes, and I found myself thinking all those old thoughts and feeling as if I was ill again, behind those walls ...

In my eagerness to travel, I also visited New Hampshire for a couple of days. Once again, I was surrounded by mountain winds soughing in the pines. You know the kind of sound I mean.

July 20, 1924
New Hampshire

Dear Second Brother,

During my 6 days here I've attended several dinners and climbed to the tops of White Mountain, Washington Mountain, Chocorua and all the peaks between them. As you can see, this letter really has come to you from deep within the mountains! We're 1,000 feet above sea level, here, and at 44 degrees latitude, which is the same bearing as the village where we used to live. The evening chill drives people away, so the only things you can see at night are the waving branches of the trees.

When Professor K invited me to come here, her letter said, I want you to experience genuine New England rural family life. And indeed, everything in the house feels as if it might really have belonged to an 18th century farming family. Old, simple walls with bricks laid by hand; oil lamps standing on the ground; rough, earthenware pottery; wild flowers on the table; at dusk, we pick up our buckets and go out to milk the cows, and gather berries to eat with our bread. These scenes aren't really much different from those we saw in the village where we lived as children. What's different is that at night beneath the lamps, everyone picks up the newspapers and discusses the Republican Party and the Democratic Party and the presidential election campaign. I feel that we Chinese are quite fortunate not to be quite so absorbed with politics. And I'm not just talking about

Chinese villages. Last year, we Chinese had no President for 40 days ... but thousands of people in Beijing nevertheless went happily on about their business. Should that make me want to laugh, or cry?

The two people who own this house are sisters, good friends of Professor K. They only live in the mountains during the summer months. I've heard that behind the mountains there's an illegal still making illicit whiskey for the neighbors, which shows you how remote and out of the way this place is. There are huge, grotesque rocks in front of the house, and behind it, too. Beyond dense clumps of trees, there are mountain ranges stretching into the distance for as far as the eye can see. Deep, dangerous gorges lurk beneath the shadows of the trees. I feel as if there must be tigers and panthers hiding in the mountains, and I never dare to walk very far. When the wind comes up rustling through the mountain grasses, I'm truly terrified that some awful, carnivorous beast will leap out at me from the dark shadows behind the trees. Even though the sisters who own the house say that the only animals here in the mountains are porcupines and small deer, I'm still wary.

As you can see, these White Mountains are very different from the Blue Mountains. The beautiful outlooks and scenic spots of the White Mountains quite surpass those of the Blue Mountains, and there are lakes everywhere; Silver Lake, Chocorua Lake, Purity Lake, and others; and the contrast of mountains and lakes is completely enchanting. One day we picnicked beside Chocorua Lake, just beyond a little bridge. There were mirror-like ripples upon the lake, and Mount Chocorua towered mightily above us. I walked up and down along the shore, enjoying the breeze from the mountain. Wherever I look I see beauty.

Other than the owners of the house and Professor K. I rarely encounter anyone else and I'm quite lonely. Alex is my only companion. He's from Newfoundland, and he's five years old. His mother works here. At bedtime on my first evening, he exclaimed: Look at that poor girl! She hasn't got her Mama to keep her company, so she's got to sleep in the little house under the trees all by herself! When I got up the next morning and the others told me about this, I felt quite moved. I smiled, but there were tears in my eyes. I've been away from Mama for a year, but this was the first time I'd heard anyone say anything so sympathetic and understanding!

I often smile at him and say: Alex, I want my Mama.

He listens attentively, thinks for a moment and then replies: I haven't seen your Mama and I don't know where she is -- maybe she's lost in the woods. Then I say: Well, I'd better go look for her. And each time I go for a walk in the woods he calls out asking: Are you going to look for your Mama?

There are lots of musical instruments and books in the house, so at first, I wasn't bored. But I do feel very lonely. There's a particular part of my life that I miss, a part of my life that I left behind in China. Do you know which part that is? It's those two or three hours of silliness and laughter we enjoyed together every day.

Floating toy battleships made of bits of iron on the water in a tub. Playing hide and seek with my little dog. Listening to you and the others telling me silly jokes you heard at school. Talking and chatting by the stove. Beating on strips of bamboo and copper bowls and singing folk-songs -- is there anyone in the world who hasn't passed happy hours doing things like this? It sounds silly, but these things are important, and necessary. I believe being able to completely relax your body and mind for a couple of hours is very beneficial and actually helps you to do serious work. It helped me to cope with anger and forget my worries, and be lively and happy. Even after I left China and didn't have much free time, there was always time for talking and joking with my companions at college and in the hospital -- we always managed to fit in a little bit of silliness. And now here I am caught between a professor and two grown ladies, quiet and reserved all day long!

But I can't start writing about all the things I remember of home! You'd love running around these wild mountains, and if I had companions, I wouldn't be so timid about exploring them. Why must I keep thinking about the past? "Past words and smiles are foolish, distant things; and it's foolish to long for what is past" But I hope that when I come back home and see everyone again after having been away for several years, you'll all remember the important things. Just let me hear your silly, foolish laughter again, and I'll be completely happy!

The mountain air is wonderful, and the sunrises and sunsets are spectacular. I'm well, mentally and physically. Just last night somebody remarked, I heard that when Tagore was in China, the students were so discourteous towards him that he fled to the Western Mountains. I simply replied, I didn't see him. Tagore is just one poet, and the fact that people met him and took him to a few places isn't that important ...

I'll stop now. But please pass this letter along to the others.

August 6, 1924
White Mountains

Every day at dusk I go to the summit of the mountain to watch the sunset and gaze at the highest peaks of Chocorua. The sides of the mountain are a light green color, but it is quite bare at the summit, with its bones showing through. It is so high, and the winds are so strong, that it's difficult for trees to grow there. The peaks of the Presidential Range zigzag along the horizon, Washington, Madison and many other mountains, piled layer upon layer and reflecting one another. I don't know why, but my favorite is Chocorua.

During a conversation at dinner, Mrs C told me that Chocorua was an American Indian chief who climbed to the top of the highest mountain and threw himself to his death because of unrequited love. Chocorua Mountain was named after him. But then she said that she didn't remember exactly how the story went, and that I'd best look it up in a book. The mountain itself seemed so heroic that I didn't like the idea of it being named after a thwarted young lover. So today I took a book called White Mountains down from the shelf and read a few pages. What it said about Chocorua's death was different from what Mrs C had told me, and I don't think there's any harm in telling you about it. The book said:

> Chocorua is considered one of the most beautiful, most picturesque of New England's high mountains. Its altitude is 3,540 feet. There is a spring at its summit, a river flowing between its peaks and a lake at its base. Among all of the mountains of New Hampshire, there is not one of comparable beauty and poetic atmosphere.
>
> Chocorua Mountain takes its name from that of an American Indian chief who was killed by white men beneath the highest peak of the mountain. There are several versions of the story. One says that after a battle at Lovewell, all of the Indians fled to Canada. However, Chocorua refused to abandon his native lands and his ancestors' graves, and stayed behind. He became friendly with the

white men, and was particularly friendly with a man named Campbell. Chocorua had only one son, so all of his love and hopes were centred upon this child. It happened that his clansmen were having an important meeting in Canada, and they asked Chocorua to attend. As he did not want his son to suffer the rigors of the journey, he entrusted the boy to Campbell, and went off by himself. The Campbell family treated Chocorua's son very well. But one day, the boy accidentally got hold of a bottle of poisonous fox-bait and drank it. When Chocorua returned, he learned that his son was dead, and had been buried. Heartbroken, anguished and not understanding what had happened, the Indian chief sought revenge. When Campbell returned from his fields, he saw the bodies of his wife and children scattered about his tent. Campbell searched frantically for Chocorua and found him on the mountain, screaming curses. Campbell threw him off the highest peak, to his death.

Another version of the story says that Chocorua was a Medicine Man, and that he and his son were very close, and that his death had nothing to do with his son's tragic death in the Campbell household. But the following version agrees with the first one.

It says that Chocorua was an innocent, unsuspecting Indian chief who was particularly amiable towards white men. But an evil, pock-marked white woman in Boston who sought Indian scalps had offered to pay $100 for each scalp, and hunters seeking this gigantic sum of money pursued the guiltless Indian chief and shot him dead at the base of the highest peak!

Just before he died, brave Chocorua opened his eyes wide and shouted a wild curse: A great disaster will befall you, white men! I ask the Great Spirit Among the Clouds to speak fiery words that will fall upon you and punish you. I have a son, and you have killed him! May lightening scorch your flesh, may violent winds and fierce fires devour your homes and families! May evil spirits breathe death upon your herds! May your graves topple and become Indian battlegrounds! May tigers, panthers, wolves and insects consume your bones! Now I go to join the Great Spirit, but my curse shall follow you forever!

The story ends there. The book goes on to say:

Afterwards, successive migrants came, but none was able to live in peace. Heaven sent calamities, one after the next; there were tempests, and pestilence; cattle and sheep died; there were Indian raids; and this continued year after year. Although the people living among nearby mountains weren't attacked by the Indians, they also found it difficult to raise livestock, and their animals continually sickened, and died. Everyone blamed Chocorua's curse. But afterwards, scientists conducted experiments and found that in fact, the drinking water was contaminated and contained large amounts of lime.

Chocorua's grave is said to be beneath the southeastern peak, but nobody has ever found it.

Every night at dusk, I go up to the mountain -- all by myself -- to watch the sunset and see the sun drop, red as fire, behind Chocorua's peaks. When all of the old, 18th century buildings are hidden among the trees all you can see are the mountain ranges, without a single trace or glimmer of civilization! At such times I try to cast my mind back a hundred years and imagine these mountains swarming with Indians running about wearing feathered headdresses. It makes me feel a little sad. The Indians are big, and their complexion is dark and beautiful, and they remind me of the Chinese. But they weren't civilized, and so they were driven away by the white man and can never return ...!

One day we went to Conway and I bought a little red clay figurine in the village shop. It's got a bright, gold crown, a green feathered headdress and colorful silk ribbons around its head and waist. I've put it on my desk and named it Chocorua as a souvenir of my posthumous admiration for Chocorua and also of my visit to the White

Mountains. I'll send him off to China at the end of the year, to wish Mama a Happy New Year for me -- I must stop, here.

August 7, 1924
White Mountains

Dear Younger Brother,

It's very early in the morning. The sun is not up, and the dew hasn't fallen. After breakfast, I must leave. Gazing dejectedly at the White Mountains, I feel that I simply must take advantage of these last hurried, silent minutes before dawn to write a short letter to you.

It was only last night, when I looked up at the Milky Way and saw the Weaving Maiden Star, that I remembered that at home, today is Double Seventh Festival Day. I thought about all the tender stories, elegant songs, and other pleasant activities that go with this holiday and are celebrated during the Festival. And here I am, wandering about in a strange land and separated from all of those things ... but let's not worry about that now!

What I intended to write about was how relatively few pleasurable, festive occasions there are for us to enjoy. True, idle holiday festivities don't make life easier, or advance our work. But pleasure is just as valuable as work. Indeed, one could even say that pleasure is part of work.

I'm not talking about mere diversions. The very word "diversion" suggests boredom, and senselessness. You seek diversions when you're bored; but when you're ill, or frustrated, you long for real pleasures, like the pleasures of festive occasions. And nations are the same as people; when they're feeling utterly disheartened, they too seek pleasure. Yes, I'll agree that some of the so-called modern pleasures seem quite dazed, confused, and listless. But I'm not writing about those! True pleasure arises from the demands of worthwhile work; in other words, when someone is engaged in a spiritually meaningful endeavor, that person is also yearning for, or creating, true pleasure.

Naturally, Chinese people yearn for Chinese pleasures, and Chinese festivals. We have over 4,000 years of stories, traditions and history. And we have twice as many holiays as other people. We begin with the New Year. Then the next holiday we celebrate is Lantern Festival. And aren't all thouse thousands of lanterns glittering beneath trees and in front of every porch magnificent! Dancing Dragon Lanterns are the ones children love most.

On the Third Day of the Third Month we celebrate the ancient Cleansing of the Riverbanks Festival. This is a good time for picnics. The flowing wine-cups and winding waters are fascinating, and remind us of the charm of ancient China. During Qing Ming Festival we sweep the graves. Even though we don't burn paper money, this Festival teaches children to respect their ancestors. If what they say about all the tree-planting that goes on during Qing Ming is true, and if everyone really does plant a seedling alongside an ancestor's grave every year, in less than a decade China will be covered with wooded, green mountains. On the Fifth Day of the Fifth Month we have a children's holiday, and everyone dresses the little ones up in fragrant, colorful silk garments. There are only a few days in the year when every child you see in every street and every lane looks so completely happy! Then there's the Dragon Boat Festival, when boats and teams from the different schools race against one another. This is also a very enjoyable day. The Seventh Day of the Seventh Month is Double Seventh Festival. It's also called Maidens' Day. Even the name has a gentle sound to it! The stars twinkle in the cool, evening breeze, melons are displayed upon the verandahs, and everyone seeks out a female companion. Amidst the quiet talk and laughter, we look up and watch the two stars as they slowly cross the Magpie Bridge and approach one another. The children's hands are full of boiled broad beans, and everyone presents them to everyone else and then we all clap our hands chanting "join your predestined soul mate"! Isn't that a wonderful expression? Mama thinks the meaning of the Chinese word"predestined" is subtle and difficult to translate. It is God's will, it is human passion, it endures through life and death, it is vast as the earth and high as the sky.

The Mid Autumn Festival takes place on the fifteenth day of the Eighth Month. And don't we all love to sit in the silvery light of the full moon and tell the tale of the Jade Hare and the Toad in the Moon! The Ninth Day of the Ninth Month is Double Ninth Festival, when our ancestors used to go out and climb the highest mountain peak they could find. Today, we just go walking around visiting scenic spots. Of course we have a National Day holiday, too. But except for the flags flying in front of the government-operated shops, it's not a holiday for family celebrations!

Well, I needn't go on. But you can find lots of other interesting, worthwhile and amusing holidays in the translations of ancient books like Western Annals. I think our Chinese festivals are more elegant than the festivals of other nations. Each one has its own, lovely story, and wonderful songs and poems, and even its own rituals and foods and emblems, like Dragon Boats and pyramid-shaped dumplings and broad beans and moon cakes and all the other festive specialties ... I won't describe them all. These traditional stories and treats and toys appeal to children, and the old poems, stories and legends provide material for the songs they sing. Our ancestors gave us these beautiful things and urged us to celebrate these noble festivals. What a shame if we fail to appreciate and enjoy them!

Certainly, getting rid of superstition is a good thing. But the saddest consequence of getting rid of superstition is that everybody then gives these lovely festivals the cold shoulder. I'm not saying you ought to be superstitious. But adults worshipping idols is one thing, while children acting out legendary stories is something quite different!

I can't write much more. The sun is up, and the cook is busy in the kitchen, preparing breakfast. Before the sun goes down this evening, I'll be on a little island. You can just imagine how pleased I am about that! Whenever I read the

Book of Odes my favorite lines are "Dark green leaves, white frost, my lord at the water's edge ... against the current, as if he was swimming." Except for my diary and letter-paper, I haven't brought any books along with me on these travels, and some of my quotations may not be correct, so please look them up. We're going to remain at the seaside until the Full Moon Festival. I'm already getting myself into the mood for "moonlight on the sea" and confess to feeling very excited about it. If I have a chance to write anything at all, I'll write to you.

August 16, 1924

Five Islands

My Dear Brothers,

Beyond the window, billows of sound and a slight trembling. It was my first night at Five Islands. I'd already gone to bed when Mrs. B came and sat on the end of the bed to have a sympathetic chat with me. "What a pity I can't bring you your Mama's smile!" she said.

It was dark by the time she left. I tossed and turned, but didn't fall asleep. Instead, I reminisced. In the middle of the year, with seas and oceans dividing us, living our lives in two separate places, wondering if life's billowing waves will ever peacefully converge... thinking such thoughts, I sighed again and again!

On my last night in New Hampshire, we celebrated

Double Seventh Festival right there in the White Mountains. Let me tell you about it, as it was quite interesting. During the day, I'd happened to mention this festival, and after I woke up from my afternoon nap, Mrs. C suggested that I change into fresh clothes. Professor K also changed out of her Western clothes, and put on an elegant Chinese outfit. Everybody else was wearing either Chinese jade pendants or Chinese silk clothing. In the twilight, surrounded by four mountains, they all sat out in front of the house underneath the tall elm trees, presenting me with tea and fruit and saying that tonight, we would celebrate the Double Seventh Festival. I couldn't help but smile. I knew that they wanted to have a bit of a party, and also, to wish me farewell. I haven't celebrated this festival at home for nearly 10 years, yet now -- thousands of li away from home, a lonely sojourner among an unbroken chain of peaks called the White Mountains, accompanied by elderly women and a university professor -- here I was, celebrating the soft, sweet, sentimental Maiden's Festival ... it was so unexpected!

According to the Lunar Calendar, that night was actually the sixth, so the two stars hadn't come together yet and the Milky Way itself was misty. Therefore, I became the centre of attention of our little gathering. They poured dandelion wine for me, and Professor K lifted her glass saying, I drink to the good fortune of every girl in China! I smiled and responded, On behalf of every girl in China, I thank you! We laughed, raised our glasses, and drank.

Next, they passed around tea and fruit. Mrs. C raised

her glass saying, With this wine, I wish you the best of health! Then the others followed suit, and Professor K and Miss E wished me good luck for the future. There was lots of friendly banter and teasing, and you could hear the loud, clear sounds of our glasses as clinked together. Everyone cheered when I smiled and drank all my wine.

We chatted until quite late, discussing modern trends and influences in poetry. After the party broke up, I considered playing a little trick upon them in the dark, but thought the better of it.

I've been here at Five Islands for nine days, and expected my thoughts to have settled down by now. Well, I was wrong! After ten years of living inland, far from the sea, I am reliving the joys of my childhood, spending mornings and evenings at the beach. My thoughts soar and I'm optimistic, not at all like my usual sober, cautious self.

During these nine days, I've helped clean the smaller boats and I've also been out on the big yacht three times. On the 13th, we had a dinner party at sea, with 16 people on board. As they hauled up the three big sails and we rode the wind, I sat alongside the railings and listened to the sound of the water and to the song the deckhands sung as they hoisted the sails, thinking of other times I'd been at sea. In the midst of my reverie, Professor B turned to me and smilingly invited me to come astern and take the tiller, saying, Try it, and let's see if you've got a navigator's blood in your veins! Everyone else on board looked at me, grinning. Carefully, I took over the tiller and sat down. My eyes were fixed upon what was right in front of me, and I also kept an eye upon the compass at my feet. The boat was small enough so that it only took one person to manage the tiller and sail it. Hanging on, I could feel the horizontal and vertical movement of the mast and its distance from the water. I relied upon my own two hands, moving the tiller and letting the boat sail on. All of my energy was concentrated upon what I was doing, and although the sea wind was blowing in my face, I didn't hear it. Gradually, we reached the mouth of Sheepcult River, where it meets the sea. The two banks of the river were rather close to one another, and the waves were turbulent. Hanging onto the tiller and holding my breath, I caught a glimpse of the other young men and women who were seated by the railing. Their faces were happy and relaxed, and they were chatting and laughing and enjoying themselves. I suddenly felt the full weight of my responsibility ... and I know this will make Papa smile! How can I possibly compare myself to Papa, who commands hundreds of warships in a mighty fleet that sails into Guangzhou Bay? Still, doing this for the very first time out there in the midst of those merciless, billowing waves, I was terrified. I'm ashamed to admit how conscious I was of the fact that the safety of those 16 lives -- male, female, young and old -- depended upon the movements of my wrists!

Professor B remained there, sitting beside me. But she didn't give me much advice, and relied upon me to come about. When we finally landed, everyone laughed and raised their hands and saluted, calling me Captain, and Mademoiselle Navigator.

This is only a frivolous thing, hardly worth mentioning. But it has made me think about Papa's twenty years at sea in an entirely new way. For the first time, I understand how it feels to assume responsibility, to take the helm. A ship is a world, and the movement of the two hands turning the wheel can be the difference between life and death, between joyful laughter and wails of sorrow. The several hundred passengers aboard an ocean liner go their leisurely, carefree way, chatting, joking, talking about braving the wind and the waves and thinking that everyone is comfortable and happy. But they don't realize that in a little room on top of the deck, the Captain is standing all alone, staring into the distance and concentrating with all his might; using all his strength and energy to protect and preserve his hundreds of passengers' carefree, merry voyage.

These are serious ideas. But the thought of spending my whole life on an island in the sea makes my mind reel. There are a couple of broken ravines at the back of the island, spanned by a little bridge. The ravines are very deep, and the waves pound through them like thunder. Making my way through the pine forest, I stand on the huge rocks looking towards the east. Spain lies out there somewhere, and there's not a speck of earth between it and me. I've sat in different places on this island, both at dawn and in the moonlight, sad and lonely -- Every night, I awaken when the tide is full and the waves are breaking beneath my window.

The foghorn from the lighthouse sounds continuously through the pale mist. Sometimes, I see silver wings swoop silently across the surface of the sea. The snowy gull's clear, penetrating cry is even more pitiful than that of the solitary wild goose. Sometimes, I wake up suddenly and then I can't get back to sleep ...

I can't put it into words, but I'm ready to leave this place, even though I know I've still got work to do, and can't come home yet.

Tomorrow on August 17th and the mail boat City of Bangor sails from Bath to Boston. I crossed the entire Pacific Ocean last year, so I can certainly manage to cross a corner of the Atlantic! Weakling though I may be, I'm not afraid to go to sea!

February 1, 1925

I've returned from the seaside and am back at the lake. The many places I've visited between there and here all seem transient as floating clouds. Half a year of my life has passed as soundlessly as slowly flowing water! I've been like a heavily laden little horse being led steadily forward, looking neither to the left nor to the right, no longer able to find the little child inside of me, and feeling a subtle, secret sorrow each time I tried to write. So I hesitated, time and again. Even so, it doesn't feel as if five whole months have passed!

Oh, dear! People tell me not to write such things to you, even though this is what I actually feel. They say I should write about more significant things, and be more constructive. How can I reply? I respect my readers and everything I've written has been simple and unaffected, clean, honest, and objective. I really have felt like a floating cloud and flowing water. I'm not being artificial, affected, or evasive. These are just the words I want to say, the words that are in my heart. Even though they may seem nihilistic, this freedom to write what I feel buoys me up and gives me the strength I'll need for the year ahead.

Last night I dreamed about a snowman, and this morning, I felt the urge to write to you. After I'd finished making the snowman in my dream, it suddenly whirled about and began to dance. When I tried to run after it, I was enveloped in a confusion of flying snowflakes. So I stood off to one side and closed my eyes, and I seemed to hear children's voices, clear and melodious, coming from within the cloud of snowflakes. The voices said, Its gone -- finished! Then I woke up. I gazed at the cold, crescent moon. In a gap between the clouds, I caught a glimpse of figures. And there was snow on the leaves, on the windowpane, even touching my hair. Disappointed, I found myself remembering an old piece of writing I'd done, called "Praise". It doesn't mean anything; it's just something I wrote. I've forgotten what it was about, and I can't even remember when I wrote it. But here it is.

A clear night at the lake, in the brilliant glow of sunset. I sit beside the water, part of this superb scene, thinking about Nature's sublime beauty, how it inspires faith. This is not only true of scenery, but of beautiful people, as well! The sight of a beautiful woman always fills me with admiration and makes me want to sing Nature's praises. The shape of an eye, an eyebrow, the curve of a waist ... among a hundred forms and shapes, these are the ones that combine to create such gentle beauty! But although lakes and mountains endure for thousands of years, the beauty of a mortal woman is ephemeral. Soulful eyes, lips like cherries, in a twinkling they are dust once more. As I made my way home through the desolate, dreary fallen leaves, I felt a deep melancholy and suddenly found myself writing these lines:

> If the ancients had an absolute standard of beauty
>> For which they praised the Creator
> Then let me worship your face
> You --
>> Your cherry-like lips encompassing all of the tenderness in the world
>> The world's wisdom condensed in your eyes.
> If I stood alone beneath the stars that night, filled with the vision
>> Of your garment, whirling plumes
>> At the side of the little boat
> If I walked alone beneath the maple trees that morning
>> Your shimmering soul
>> Seemed almost to appear beside me!

I need only clasp my hands and bow my head
    Wordlessly
    For you are Nature
    Goddess ...
Now you can use fairies' magic
    Encased in mortal flesh and blood
Dignified
    Sitting opposite me in the silvery lamplight
I worship you silently
    Secretly, admiring
    With all my heart
Sighing, smiling one!
    Thanks to you I praise the omnipotent Creator of
all
    Sighing, smiling one!
    Step by step, you have led me along the road to
belief in the Divine.
    I worship you silently
    With all my heart
Sighing, smiling one!
You need only gaze down through those deep, limpid, wise
eyes
    To see falling leaves everywhere, all over the world
    Next year, when spring comes
    New, green buds will again appear on the ancient
branches
    Sighing, smiling one!
    Youth is gone

You know you are not its equal!
Cherry-like lips, gazing eyes, are but traces of a dream
In tenderness and in wisdom, immortal You!

October 7, 1925
Medford

I'm most likely to write when I'm ill, or when it's very quiet, or when it's raining. Illness makes me melancholy. When it's quiet, my mind becomes quite cool and fresh. And when it rains, my head fills with mysterious thoughts. I need only take up my pen at such times, and I can write pages and pages.

After a whole summer's wanderings, all I want to do now is rest. Beyond the window, a light rain is falling, and I sit here watching the flames in the hearth. I've read so much that I'm sick of reading, and have turned off the lamp that stands beside my chair. Bits of firewood crackle and burst one after the next, and sparks fly out of the stove onto the edges of my skirt -- Oh, dear! I'm bored silly, with the quiet and the rain! And after all these weeks of silence, here I am writing to you again!

On the morning of June 18th, while the sky was still overcast and before it had become too warm, I hurriedly took the pots of flowers growing in my room and transplanted them beneath the trees. Respectfully, I asked the wind and the rain to protect next year's flowers for the next person who'll come here and sit reading at my little

table. Finding a safe place for my beloved pot plants had
been worrying me! Afterwards, I traveled by train for a day
and a night to Silver Bay.

What a musical name! It reminds me of a line of
poetry. Sailing into the bay, one sees hillsides and green
mountains surrounding Lake George, layer upon layer of
green. A clump of trees upon a little island is so bright and
brilliant that it would open the eyes of even the most jaded
traveler. Bit by bit, Silver Bay unfolds before my eyes. The
Black Mountains are very high, and Lake George is truly
enormous, and the huge waves that roar against the foot of
the mountains give Silver Bay a distinctly artistic aura.

After I arrived I sent a postcard to a friend, saying:
It's difficult for a person to live up to a high reputation, so
why should it be any different for a place? You said Silver
Bay was like paradise, but having traveled extensively, I find
it rather ordinary! -- for indeed, "poets become accustomed
to the exceptional, and their fantasies soar too high!" To tell
you the truth, having seen the deep blue sea, Silver Bay --
vast and picturesque though it may be --isn't all that
outstanding. In fact, it's not even as beautiful as secluded,
charming, Lake Waban, where I was moved to write poems
of praise.

But I shall put all of my preconceived ideas aside, and
tell you about some of Silver Bay's nicest scenic spots. Brook
Pavilion is built upon a distant rocky outcrop, and
surrounded by water on three sides. When I get up early in
the morning and sit there reading poetry, the sound of the

murmuring water seems to rhyme with the tones of the poems. Showers often sweep down from the mountains and just before it starts to rain, everything looks exceptionally vivid as the clouds' reflections glide slowly across the surface of the lake. After the rain passes the lake is as clear as a mirror, and the green mountains look as if they've just been scrubbed. Resplendent rays of shining morning sunshine gleam through gaps in the clouds and penetrate the water with light, its reflections blending into an endless, seamless series of rainbows. The exotic beauty of this scene is a challenge to a poet, for it is beyond description!

There's nothing I'd have liked better than to sit in a boat on the lake and write letters, but unfortunately, there wasn't time. However, on the afternoon of the 26th, I did take the boat through white waves to the other side of the lake, where I managed to write a few lines. It's a huge lake, over three miles across! The wind was very strong when I returned, and the boat rose and fell, and the letter I'd written blew away somewhere in the middle of the lake. I was rowing against the ebbing tide, and I felt quite proud of how well I did. But after I got back, both of my arms ached a bit.

Ten days later, we went back to Ithaca..

Ithaca is so beautiful! with many lovely, peaceful locations. The people were like hermits, the weather like autumn, the flowers like chrysanthemums. It was the first time I'd ever stayed so near to a spring, and quite a novelty. There were deep ravines everywhere among the trees. I could even hear the sound of the spring in my dreams at night! During the sixty days that I spent traveling and touring, I continually felt as if "all sorts of feelings surged in my soul and my body was like a sponge, absorbing everything".

I sat and read alongside the spring, next to the path that winds beneath the cliff. There are simply no words in the language that would truly describe this place for you -- Americans come here during the summer. In Ithaca I even wandered around a graveyeard! A profoundly silent place like this is quite philosophical, and makes you think deeply about life, and death. I went back there three times during the week, stroking the gravestones and plucking the last flowers. I felt the people buried here were serene and at peace, and I wondered what they might be thinking of me.

Lake Canuga is famous for its beautiful scenery, and we often went boating there. The lake it very large, but its scenic spots weren't as lovely as Lake Waban, and I won't bother writing about them.

On August 28th we visited Niagara Falls. The silvery waves swept to and fro past Three Sisters Rock, battering the rock with a sound like horses' hooves and surging into a whirlpool of turbulent, heaving billows hidden beneath an unhurried flow of tiny ripples. I rode straight to the base of the waterfall in a little boat named Maid of the Mist. Looking up at the United States on one side of the gigantic torrent and Canada on the other side, I could practically reach out and touch the heavy, cottony clouds that engulfed our boat. The setting sun turned the reflections in the water to a deep blue color, the waves smashed against the rocks and droplets of water clung to my head-scarf. The thundering noise of the torrent made my soul throb with fear. The magnificent colors had a deep, profound, tenderly gently beauty, rejoicing in this mighty, cold, cleansing torrent of water. We returned that evening in the moonlight, suddenly feeling oddly lost.

We arrived in Syracuse on September 2nd, in the rain, to attend the annual meeting of Chinese Students in the Eastern United States. This year, the theme was Nationalism and China, and everyone had their say.

I spent 10 days at the Annual Conference, and then returned to Boston. On the evening of the 14th, my thoughts still speeding like the wheels of a chariot, the splendid lamps of Boston's South Station suddenly awakened me from those ten days' of dreams and imaginings ...

It's already quite dark and my hosts are urging me to go to bed. Outside the window, it's still raining. The voices of foreign insects call bleakly. From 10,000 li away, I wish my readers goodnight!

March 12, 1926

As I had no reason to go to the function at Wheaton College, yesterday afternoon I went to Mansfield.

When I reached the station and looked at my ticket, I realized that one must pass through Sharon when one travels from Boston to Mansfield. Suddenly, a nameless listlessness gripped me!

Since leaving Sharon, I'd already been back twice to visit the friends I'd made there. Both times, it was frustrating. I was nervous, forcing myself to smile whenever there was a silence. Gazing at the fallen leaves and dead branches alongside the road, each twig and leaf reminded me of my battle against illness! But this time I wasn't going all the way to Sharon and although I was trying to be objective, I couldn't repress a heartfelt sigh! I remembered that from the hospital's front verandah you could just manage to see the distant white wisps of smoke from passing trains through a gap in the treetops. I remembered the exact spot and as I stared attentively into the distance, I could see the hospital's snow-covered roof, set off in the slanting rays of the setting sun like a jade palace ...

I awoke from my dreams at 7 AM at dawn, and saw it again! Enjoying the spring weather, the newly-risen sun and the sight of the returning migratory birds, I remembered that on this day just a year ago I was standing on the mountain road in my windblown spring clothes! How time seemed to stop!

Tell me, what is illness? Does it cause these sorts of shocks? I often ask myself this question. And friends who haven't seen me for years say I've changed. I'm not saying I'd have necessarily become something different in a different place, yet I don't seem to be the same person after my illness. What if this is true? Is it fortunate, or unfortunate? Either way, it's worth thinking about.

Yesterday, after I'd returned and had a rest, I felt disappointed with myself and sorry that I hadn't sent you a letter. During the evening, I sat beneath the lamp rummaging through all of the letters that you sent me during my illness. And I can tell you, I didn't know which was worse, victory or defeat. There were suddenly so many things I wanted to say that I couldn't bear it.

Have you ever seen a strong man wrestle with a lion? Holding his breath and struggling with all his might, his empty fists pitted against savage teeth and claws, he may be shaking with terror or maddened with pride, but he's so wrapped up in what's happening that he hasn't time to feel sorrow or despair. But when the strength and spirit that came to him during the struggle have abated, when the king of beasts has been dispatched beyond the iron gates of death, his thoughts are weary and muddled as he sits dejectedly upon the lion's head. Amidst the thunder of cheering voices he looks up tremulously at the mane and tail and the trees above his head and he himself seems like a huge beast, gasping for breath. I think he must suddenly begin to tremble and shudder unbearably, his whole body becoming so soft and weak it seems about to vanish beneath the waves of a lonely sea.

It goes without saying that someone who has suffered a crushing defeat is distraught, and will groan with pain! But such emotional outbursts are spontaneous rather than profound, and can't be controlled. Even the warrior who has aimed too high and must eventually withdraw feels a surge of emotion when he visits his former battleground. He stands there like a bereft ghost in the waning light of day, motionless with listlessness and reverie. Alone beneath the setting sun.the gray-haired old veteran of a hundred successful battles cannot accept this quiet desolation. How sad it is, the sorrow of the victor!

With what courage and joy did I struggle against illness! I felt like a child, like an Eskimo. My "feet trod upon dry twigs, and in the silence I heeded the whispered language of the leaves ... I tried to lift the curtain of Mother Nature's own sepulcher and tiptoe into her Fairy Palace!" And now all of that is past! "All day long I am reserved, my head lowered over my needlework ... I've let a year pass soundlessly, like flowing water." And it's true, "having returned to the road of health, a thousand day to day cares are already following at my heels!" But I want to say this to Mama: Now that I really understand life, I appreciate it more than ever. I want to taste each and every one of life's delights, and I want to savor each of them to the full! --- I am more than willing to "use the blood and tears of illness as a sacrifice to open the gates of the Kingdom of Life" And I want to say this to my readers: Appreciate life! Be like a needle thrusting through felt! Use your mortal flesh and blood to seek out every sorrow and every delight, let your needle draw blood! --For as I tell my readers, who knows what the future will hold when you're grown up? Every delight in a life in which "each stitch draws blood" must be purchased with a bit of simple, childlike innocence. What costs must be paid for the experiences to come? I don't know. But I have changed, and I can tell you -- readers and Mama, too -- that from now on, I shall willingly submit to whatever life demands of me. Even so, I still hope you'll listen to me when I'm weak and defeated and sorrowful!

Now that you faithful, enthusiastic readers have allowed me to get all of that off my chest, let me tell you some news that will please everyone. In the Eastern Hemisphere, Mama is now counting the months, because in just four more months, we'll all be together again! So don't bother feeling sympathetic because of the letters I wrote before January, for they are merely blown blossoms! How happy I am now!

But I apologize, too. For once again, I've confided all my sorrowful thoughts to you. But my poetic muse is "soft, gentle and a little bit afraid" so it's good to let her express herself this way.

July 30, 1926
Shanghai

Dearest Mama,

This morning, I received the book of my collected letters that Bing sent from Beijing. I looked through it hurriedly, bubbling with enthusiasm. Dearest Mama! I've already set foot upon the earth of my native land, and my heart is filled with joy and relief and also a little sadness. I find myself remembering that Sunday three years ago, as I stood with my hand upon the ship's railing, sailing away into the dusk. I remember how the cool breeze blowing up from the surface of the river made me think of you. Three years later, nothing has changed. I'm still your daughter, the same daughter you held in your arms all those years ago!

Shanghai is wretchedly hot. I find myself thinking about the sea breezes, and the bright moonlight. Truly, everything passes! I remember our sixth night at sea on the way home, with the roaring waves and the deep, black water and only the moonlight separating us, paving the surface of the water with a shining, bright road of broken light. Gazing at the bright, splashing waves hitting the side of the ship, all my dreams of traveling to faraway places burst like bubbles. Mama, you are the sea and I am the moment between the leap and the splash of a wave. The wave gleams and glitters for a moment, but in the twinkling of an eye it flings itself back into Mama's arms. I'm already stretching myself and yawning after my beautiful dream of travel! Waves from my native land call to me one after the next and wash away the dream images. People in dreams are only make-believe, but your soul and mine are linked together, forever!

I remember that on the seventh morning, I woke up before dawn but after I'd seen the shapes of Chinese sails on the river in the distance, I couldn't sleep another wink! Through the porthole, I watched the full moon sinking in the west, its violet light fading. The bright, morning glow on the eastern horizon had already told me it would soon be daylight. Mama, your daughter (returned from her 10,000 li journey to foreign lands) has always been moved by the sight of the setting moon and the morning sunlight, but the sight of them today fills her soul with endless love and admiration.

I'm a child of the hills and mountains and seaboard, a child of the wild, northern countryside. I couldn't bear to live in Shanghai! Long skirts, short shirts, butterfly-wing sleeves, shiny, oiled hair, wispy fringes cut on foreheads. There are a thousand people on this ship and and none of them powder their faces, which makes me cross, and also a bit timid. Things are very hectic, and everyone seems to want to fill me up with wine. Last night we drank Great Winding Fragrance wine, which wasn't bad, but tonight, I got tipsy on something called White Rose Dew. I hurried upstairs and lay down on the bed without even undressing. We'd been drinking until midnight, and now, moonlight came through my window. In its dim glow I remembered that my "abandoned home" was very near, and thus warded off sorrowful feelings of "poplars and willows, dawn winds, waning moon."

My writing is so uneven that you'll think I'm still drunk! I sail north on August 2nd, in the evening. Dearest Mama! Even thought I fear that I still can't drink wine, it's good to be home!

August, 31,1926
Yuanenshi

I'm home! What happy tears of gratitude fill my eyes when I say that one small word! I think about my three years under a foreign sun, and decide I might just as well ponder the passing waves. As I write this letter, my little brother Bing Ji is standing guard beside me. When I look out the window, I see red, sweet-scented oleander and green willows and poplars, set off against Bejing's azure sky. Day after day, the scenic beauties of my homeland unfold before my eyes!

Dear friends! If you've never left north China and been away for three whole years, the azure blue skies of the north won't make you gasp with admiration and appreciation. Rising at dawn, opening the curtains and looking out at this vast expanse of blue sky, with spotlessly white clouds floating before your eyes and the willow leaves swaying gently in the dawn breezes makes you feel a delicious coolness, a unique sense of atmosphere that you never feel in foreign lands, no matter how hard you try! If you're an emotional, self-conscious, introspective person, you may sometimes find that certain pleasures make you incredibly happy while certain disappointments seem very cruel and make you quite miserable, so that unintended tears may follow hard upon wildly unreasonable hopes!

I only saw a sky like this twice while I was overseas. Once was a year ago, among the peaks of the White Mountains of New Hampshire, on a summer afternoon. I'd just got up from a nap. A letter had arrived for me from an English friend, full of thoughts about friendship and other things. Concentrating upon her descriptions and perspiring in the heat of the afternoon, I fell into a sort of dreamlike mood. Feeling both dejected and happy, I walked outside, still holding the letter. Suddenly, I realized that this foreign sky was as blue as the sea! Set off by the colors of the mountains that surrounded me, its dense, azure blue permeated everything. The setting sun filled the sky. On the Western horizon, two daubs of a deep reddish purple color appeared. Instant by instant the colors changed, now silvery gray, now white, and then in the twinkling of an eye, splendid gold. The mountains were still, and it seemed as if the very universe was speaking in these astonishing, fluctuating heavens. Like the surge of a wave, like a bird's cry upon the wind, I seemed to hear the sound of the setting sun. And then I became aware of my own, small self; feeling as if I'd been raised up to Heaven and plummeted down to the bottom of the sea at the same time! Aware of Nature's grandeur, surrounded on all four sides by natural beauty, I was overwhelmed, and fell down onto the soft grass sobbing as if I'd never stop.

The second time was a spring day this year, one evening in Washington. I'd traveled south from the dry, cold city of New York, and discovered that in Washington, it was already spring! It was dusk, and I was sitting by a window in a building just opposite the White House, enjoying the gentle breeze. My eyes were tired after half a day's sight-seeing, but the evening sky was amazing! All of you on the other side of the world, accept my apologies! I'd been living in the United States for over two years before I saw the White House, but in all that time, I'd never thought of America as a dignified country. All day, the White House towered before my eyes like the exquisite palace of an Immortal. The brilliant light coming from the powerful lamps at the sides of the building made the black void beyond seem even blacker. There were huge, white stone buildings on either side. And in front, a wide boulevard made of white stone. The dazzling round, white lamps cast a steady light. In the midst of this vast panorama, the pedestrians on the footpaths were silent. This was the first time since I'd been in America that I'd encountered this reverent observation of silence. Thus I discovered that they have the same kinds of places in Washington as we have in Beijing!

I was suddenly so overwhelmed by feelings of homesickness that it was like being capsized in a billowing, angry sea. I pushed back my chair, left the tall, silent building and made my way to the National Library. As I walked, an inexpressible feeling of happiness and freedom came over me. The fresh, green poplars and willows swayed in the breezes of the early spring evening. I went into the Main Reading Room and sat down and began to write in my journal, just like a habitual visitor. Writing reminded me of some lines from a poem by Lu Fang Weng:

Master! I was your guest
And did not force my way into the building.

As I pondered the meaning of these lines, I gradually became sad again. Closing my journal, I left the building. Outside beneath the star-studded sky, I gave a long sigh --- At the side of the road, I saw a black man pushing a wheelbarrow and calling out that he had roasted chestnuts for sale. I hadn't eaten snacks between meals since before I became ill, but I promptly stopped and bought some chestnuts from him. That dark, amiable face smiling at me beneath the lamps made me once again think yearningly of home! How I'd longed for chestnuts! More than ever, Washington reminded me of Beijing!

My wrist is weak from having written so much. I don't know if I should tell you this, but after I got home, I was ill for over a week. This morning was the first time I felt well enough to write a letter. I was already run down and tired out from all my traveling, and after I got home I was so relaxed that sickness seized the opportunity and pounced. I never really thought about the possibility of being ill again. I don't know why, for throughout this whole correspondence, hasn't my life usually been a combination of ordinary life mixed with illness?

Here at home, it's early autumn. Recuperating, I feel a joyous rustling in the air! There are still so many things to say, but they'll keep until later. I'll leave you now.

Wishing you great happiness, I remain your enthusiastic, faithful friend,

43232623R00122

Made in the USA
Charleston, SC
18 June 2015